# First Workshop on Computing News Storylines

# (CNewsStory 2015)



**Co-located with ACL-IJCNLP 2015**

## Beijing, China
## 31 July 2015

ISBN: 978-1-5108-0952-9

**Printed from e-media with permission by:**

Curran Associates, Inc.
57 Morehouse Lane
Red Hook, NY 12571

**Some format issues inherent in the e-media version may also appear in this print version.**



Printed by Curran Associates, Inc. (2015)



Association for Computational Linguistics
209 N. Eighth Street
Stroudsburg, Pennsylvania 18360

Phone: 1-570-476-8006
Fax: 1-570-476-0860

acl@aclweb.org

**Additional copies of this publication are available from:**

Curran Associates, Inc.
57 Morehouse Lane
Red Hook, NY 12571 USA
Phone: 845-758-0400
Fax: 845-758-2634
Email: curran@proceedings.com
Web: www.proceedings.com

ACL-IJCNLP 2015

# Proceedings of the First Workshop on Computing News Storylines (CNewsStory 2015)

July 31, 2015
Beijing, China

# Introduction

This volume contains the proceedings of the 1st Workshop on Computing News Storylines (CNewsStory 2015) held in conjunction with the 53rd Annual Meeting of the Association for Computational Linguistics and the 7th International Joint Conference on Natural Language Processing (ACL-IJCNLP 2015) at the China National Convention Center in Beijing, on July 31st 2015.

Narratives are at the heart of information sharing. Ever since people began to share their experiences, they have connected them to form narratives. The study of storytelling and the field of literary theory called narratology have developed complex frameworks and models related to various aspects of narrative such as plots structures, narrative embeddings, characters' perspectives, reader response, point of view, narrative voice, narrative goals, and many others. These notions from narratology have been applied mainly in Artificial Intelligence and to model formal semantic approaches to narratives (e.g. Plot Units developed by Lehnert (1981)). In recent years, computational narratology has qualified as an autonomous field of study and research. Narrative has been the focus of a number of workshops and conferences (AAAI Symposia, Interactive Storytelling Conference (ICIDS), Computational Models of Narrative). Furthermore, reference annotation schemes for narratives have been proposed (NarrativeML by Mani (2013)).

The majority of the previous work on narratives and narrative structures have mainly focused on the analysis of fictitious texts. However, modern day news reports still reflect this narrative structure, but they have proven difficult for automatic tools to summarise, structure, or connect to other reports. This difficulty is partly rooted in the fact that most text processing tools focus on extracting relatively simple structures from the local lexical environment, and concentrate on the document as a unit or on even smaller units such as sentences or phrases, rather than cross-document connections. However, current information needs demand a move towards multidimensional and distributed representations which take into account the connections between all relevant elements involved in a "story". Additionally, most work on cross-document temporal processing focuses on linear timelines, i.e. representations of chronologically ordered events in time (for instance, the Event Narrative Event Chains by Chambers (2011), or the SemEval 2015 Task 4: Cross Document TimeLines by Minard et al. (2014)). Storylines, though, are more complex, and must take into account temporal, causal and subjective dimensions. How storylines should be represented and annotated, how they can be extracted automatically, and how they can be evaluated are open research questions in the NLP and AI communities.

The workshop aimed to bring together researchers from different communities working on representing and extracting narrative structures in news, a text genre which is highly used in NLP but which has received little attention with respect to narrative structure, representation and analysis. Currently, advances in NLP technology have made it feasible to look beyond scenario-driven, atomic extraction of events from single documents and work towards extracting story structures from multiple documents, while these documents are published over time as news streams. Policy makers, NGOs, information specialists (such as journalists and librarians) and others are increasingly in need of tools that support them in finding salient stories in large amounts of information to more effectively implement policies, monitor actions of "big players" in the society and check facts. Their tasks often revolve around reconstructing cases either with respect to specific entities (e.g. person or organizations) or events (e.g. hurricane Katrina). Storylines represent explanatory schemas that enable us to make better selections of relevant information but also projections to the future. They form a valuable potential for exploiting news data in an innovative way.

Albeit small in number, the contributions that are published in this volume do indeed cover the topics we intended to touch upon. We received 12 submissions and accepted 9. Two papers focus on tracking and representing emergent news topics (Tadashi) and develop personalised news aggregation systems (Fedorovsky et al.). Events, the primary source of information and blocks for storylines, are the targets of three papers which tackles different issues such as improving event type detection (Li et al.), the analysis of the properties of sequences of events (Simonson and Davis), and the automatic extraction of news agendas as the ability of storylines to direct action (Stalpouskaya and Baden). Notions such as relevance and importance are at the core of two papers: one paper which describes a formal model and a preliminary implementation for automatically extracting storylines from news stream (Vossen et al.), and one paper which proposes a post-retrieval snippet clustering based on pattern structures (Makhalova et al.). Finally, a proposal for storyline representation and evaluation (Laparra et al.) and the adaptation of approaches and methods from the domain of fiction to the news data (Miller et al.) are reported.

We would like to thank the members of the Program Committee for their timely reviews. We would also like to thank the authors for their contributions.

**Organizers:**

Tommaso Caselli, VU University Amsterdam
Marieke van Erp, VU University Amsterdam
Anne-Lyse Minard, Fondazione Bruno Kessler
Mark Finlayson, Florida International University
Ben Miller, Georgia State University
Jordi Atserias, Yahoo! Barcelona
Alexandra Balahur, European Commission's Joint Research Centre
Piek Vossen, VU University Amsterdam

**Program Committee:**

Sabine Bergler, Concordia University, Canada
Matje van de Camp, De Taalmonsters, The Netherlands
Erik van der Goot, EC Joint Research Centre, Italy
Nathanael Chambers, United States Naval Academy, USA
Leon Derczynski, University of Sheffield, UK
Anthony Jameson, DFKI, Germany
Bernardo Magnini, Fondazione Bruno Kessler, Italy
Jarred McGinnis, Logomachy.org, UK
Roser Morante, VU University Amsterdam, The Netherlands
Silvia Pareti, Google Inc. & University of Edinburgh
Ellen Riloff, University of Utah, USA
Roser Saurí, Pompeu Fabra University, Spain
Hristo Tanev, EC Joint Research Centre, Italy
Xavier Tannier, Université Paris-Sud & LIMSI-CNRS, France
Naushad UzZanam, Nuance Communications, Inc.
Laure Vieu, IRIT-CNRS - Université Toulouse III, France
Marc Verhagen, Brandeis University, USA

# Table of Contents

# Conference Program

**31 July 2015**

**09:15–09:25** ***Opening Remarks***



**10:30–11:00** ***Coffee Break***



**12:30–14:00** ***Lunch Break***



**14:40–15:30** ***Discussion and Conclusions***

# Interactions between Narrative Schemas and Document Categories

**Dan Simonson**
Department of Linguistics
Georgetown University
Washington, DC, 20057, USA
des62@georgetown.edu

**Anthony R. Davis**
Enterra Solutions
Silver Spring, MD, 20910, USA
tonydavis0@gmail.com

## Abstract

The unsupervised extraction of *narrative schemas*—sets of events with associated argument chains—has been explored and evaluated from many angles (Chambers and Jurafsky, 2009; Jans et al. 2012; Balasubramanian et al., 2013; Pichotta and Mooney 2014). While the extraction process and evaluation of the products has been well-researched and debated, little insight has been garnered on properties of narrative schemas themselves. We examine how well extracted narrative schemas align with existing document categories using a novel procedure for retrieving candidate category alignments. This was tested against alternative baseline alignment procedures that disregard some of the complex information the schemas contain. We find that a classifier built with all available information in a schema is more precise than a classifier built with simpler subcomponents. Coreference information plays an crucial role in schematic knowledge.

## 1 Introduction

In this work, we examine the properties of narrative schemas—sets of events linked by common participants. Though they've been widely investigated, little work has been done to deploy schemas as a component of a larger NLP task, aside from tasks devised purely for validating schemas. To understand what tasks are best suitable for narrative schemas, we've begun to look closely at their properties with the aim of applying them to other NLP tasks.

Intuitively, narrative schemas are plausibly and implicitly linked to the notion of a document category—that is, a schema can represent the narrative commonalities shared by a set of documents. In this work, we set out to try to substantiate this claim in two different ways: we investigate the relationship between schemas and topics and we attempt to use these distributions to classify a set of documents. In Section (2), we describe the variety of techniques that have been attempted to create schemas. In Section (3), we describe the selection criteria for our source data. In Section (4), we discuss our schema extraction procedure, mostly derived from prior work with a few variations. In Section (5), we discuss how categories are assigned to schemas. In Section (6), we outline our different baseline and classifier experiments, and in Sections (7) and (8), we present the results of our experiments. In Sections (9) and (10), we wrap up with implications of these results for future work.

## 2 Background

What are referred to as *schemas*, *templates*, or *frames* were first introduced in Schank and Abelson (1977) as a generalization of recurring event knowledge. They present scripts as a theory of human memory—events that occur enough are generalized into a script by some aspect of the human mind.

Chambers and Jurafsky (2008; 2009) developed and implemented techniques for the automatic extraction of schemas. A number of papers presenting alternatives, innovations, and variants have followed. Some use co-referent argument pairs—a combination of coreference and syntactic parses to obtain counts of verb-dependency pairs that share a coreferent (Chambers and Jurafsky, 2008;



*Proceedings of the First Workshop on Computing News Storylines*, pages 1–10,
Beijing, China, July 31, 2015. 

Chambers and Jurafsky, 2009; Chambers, 2013; Jans et al. 2012; Pichotta and Mooney 2014). Others focus on how the information is presented in a given text, eschewing coreference information altogether to build schemas based on its structure alone (Cheung, Poon, and Vandervende 2013; Balasubramanian et al., 2013). These schemas contain knowledge not of which actors are likely to participate in which actions but of which events are like to occur before and after one another in prose.

In addition to a choice between textual or coreference information providing the basis for scoring, the interactions between different role slots across verbs are handled in roughly two different ways. One approach is to train on individual verb-dependency pairs, themselves associating arguments to verbs (Chambers and Jurafsky, 2008; Chambers and Jurafsky, 2009; Chambers, 2013; Jans et al. 2012). On the other hand, all role fillers can be handled together as one tuple that acts as the argument to a verb (Pichotta and Mooney 2014; Balasubramanian et al., 2013). The key difference is that the verb-dependency approach accepts arguments to a particular verb without giving those arguments any information about the others; the tuple approach informs the arguments about one another in some way. Verb-dependency approaches are more Davidsonian in the degree of freedom given to verb arguments than their tuple-bound counterparts (Davidson 1967).

Candidate insertions into a schema are ranked in different ways. Pointwise mutual information ($pmi$) is used in a number of approaches (Chambers and Jurafsky, 2008; Chambers and Jurafsky, 2009; Jans et al. 2012) or maximization of probability given features under consideration, including argument types and verb collocations themselves (Jans et al. 2012; Pichotta and Mooney 2014). Balasubramanian et al. (2013) use a graph-ranking algorithm to generate schemas. Some newer work takes a more theoretically sophisticated approach, employing a formal probabilistic model along with a Hidden Markov Model to induce schematic knowledge (Chambers, 2013; Cheung, Poon, and Vandervende 2013).

Most implementations have been evaluated using the narrative cloze task (Chambers and Jurafsky, 2008; Chambers and Jurafsky, 2009; Jans et al. 2012; Pichotta and Mooney 2014). In this procedure, a random verb is removed from a document and the previously extracted schematic knowledge is used to rank alternative verbs that could fill the empty event slot. Balasubramanian et al. (2013)—contrary to other approaches—use human intuitions from Amazon Mechanical Turk to evaluate their schemas.

## 3 Data Selection

Our data came entirely from the New York Times Corpus (Sandhaus 2008), which consists of around 1.8 million documents from the eponymous newspaper. Each document comes tagged with associated metadata, including date, two types of document categories, tags of people mentioned in each document, and other information.

From the original 1.8 million documents, 38832 were retained to generate schemas after our selection process, described next.

### 3.1 Keyword and Year Selection

All documents containing the keyword "police" in any form were extracted from the New York Times Corpus. Documents from late 1994 to mid 2008 were retained. This reduced the set to roughly 8% of the original corpus size.

### 3.2 Categorical Selection

Documents in the NYT corpus are tagged with an `online_producer` property that provides categorical labels for documents. A subset of these categories was then retained, with the intention of providing not only a variety of narratives, but also some more potentially complex distinctions that could be difficult to disentangle. Collectively, this represents a set of documents that are more likely to refer to police as the focus—"noise" and "demonstrations and riots"—than many of those excluded—"international relations" and "United States Armament and Defense." No categories outside of this set were explicitly excluded, however, and nothing prevents these categories from overlapping, which they often do. Most extreme in this regard is the category "Serial Murders", where every article is also contained in "Murders and Attempted Murders."

In total, 38832 documents remain in the corpus of source data. Table (1) lists the categories and gives a breakdown of the distribution of documents across categories.

### 3.3 Coreference and Dependency Preparation

Documents were parsed and their coreference chains were extracted with Stanford CoreNLP version 3.4.1 (Manning et al. 2014), particularly the Stanford Parser (de Marneffe, MacCartney, and Manning 2006) and the Stanford Deterministic Coreference Resolution System (Lee et al. 2013). From the parser, we used the `collapsed-ccprocessed-dependencies`. We only looked at dependencies related to the verb, and each dependency was collapsed into an appropriate super-category: `agent`, `subj`, `nsubj`, `csubj`, `xsubj` are all mapped to `SUBJ`; `comp`, `obj`, `dobj`, `nsubjpass` to `OBJ`; `iobj` and `prep_.*` to `PREP`.[1]

## 4 Extracting Schemas

In this section, we discuss in detail two components of how we created schemas. The first is how we scored candidate events for adding to a particular schema, with our score being largely derived from Chambers and Jurafsky (2009). In the second, we discuss how this score is used to generate schemas.

### 4.1 Scoring Candidate Events

We largely followed Chambers and Jurafsky (2009) in scoring candidate events with respect to a particular schema.

Their score is based on *pmi*, defined in this context as:

$$pmi(\langle w,d\rangle,\langle v,g\rangle) = \log \frac{P(\langle w,d\rangle,\langle v,g\rangle)}{P(\langle w,d\rangle)P(\langle v,g\rangle)} \quad (1)$$

where $w$ and $v$ are verbs, $d$ and $g$ are dependencies. The probabilities $P$ of pairs of narrative events are defined as:

$$P(\langle w,d\rangle,\langle v,g\rangle) = \frac{C(\langle w,d\rangle,\langle v,g\rangle)}{\sum_{w',v'}\sum_{d',f'} C(\langle w',d'\rangle,\langle v',f'\rangle)} \quad (2)$$

where $C(\langle w,d\rangle,\langle v,g\rangle)$ is the number of times a co-reference chain contains some word that has $d$ dependency with verb $w$ and some word that has a $g$ dependency with verb $v$. For example, the pair of sentences "John$_i$ danced poorly. The crowd booed at him$_i$" would contribute one count to $C(\langle \texttt{dance, SUBJ}\rangle,\langle \texttt{boo, PREP}\rangle)$.

[1] Chambers and Jurafsky (2009) include *prep* as one of their argument slots but do not include it in their diagrams: "An *event slot* is a tuple of an event and a particular argument slot (grammatical relation), represented as a pair $\langle v,d\rangle$ where $v$ is a verb and $d \in \{subject, object, prep\}$."

To include the effect of typed arguments, (Chambers and Jurafsky, 2009) defines $sim$ as:

$$sim(\langle e,d\rangle,\langle e',d'\rangle,a) = pmi(\langle e,d\rangle,\langle e',d'\rangle) + \lambda \log freq(\langle e,d\rangle,\langle e',d'\rangle,a) \quad (3)$$

$a$ represents a specific argument type. $freq(b,b',a)$ returns the corpus count of $a$ filling both $b$ and $b'$.

Chambers and Jurafsky (2009) used an open set of noun phrase heads to generate their types. Instead, we created an explicit list of preferred types from the top 300 tokens contained in noun phrases. We then removed cardinal numbers from this candidate list, leaving 294 preferred argument types. This was done for two reasons: to reduce data sparsity and to improve performance since $chainsim'$ maximizes over all possible types.

If none of the preferred types are available inside any of the noun phrases of a co-reference chain, the results from the Stanford NER (Finkel, Grenager, and Manning 2005) are checked. After this, any pronouns are used to map a coreference chain to an appropriate fall-back type, either `SELF`, `PERSON`, `THING` or `PEOPLE` as appropriate. If there is no obtainable type, a final fall-back called `THINGY` is used.

Chambers and Jurafsky (2009) point out that $sim$ biases the selection of verbs in favor of adding a new verb that simply shares an argument type with another verb already in the schema. However, this does not guarantee that the type works for all events already in the schema. For this reason, $score$ is defined as follows, to sum over $sim$ values with all current elements of the schema:

$$score(C,a) = \sum_{i=1}^{n-1}\sum_{j=i+1}^{n} sim(\langle e_i,d_i\rangle,\langle e_j,d_j\rangle,a) \quad (4)$$

With $sim$ and $score$, $chainsim'$ is defined as:

$$chainsim'(C,\langle f,g\rangle) = \max_a \left( score(C,a) + \sum_{i=1}^{n} sim(\langle e_i,d_i\rangle,\langle f,g\rangle,a) \right) \quad (5)$$

$chainsim'$ superpositions the influence of two forces on introducing a new pair $\langle f,g\rangle$ to a chain: how well $\langle f,g\rangle$ fits in the chain—which constitutes $\sum sim(...)$—and how well the argument $a$ fits within the context of the rest of the chain—the effect of the $score(C, a)$ component. $chainsim'$ finds the best argument for inducing this combination.

Differing from Chambers and Jurafsky, the candidate verb argument type $a$ that maximized $score$ in Formula (5) is also retained to add to the list of types associated with that chain in the schema. If a role slot fails to score higher than a threshold for any existing chains in the schema, a new, un-filled singleton chain is started. If no evidence for a slot was observed in the data with respect to a particular verb, that slot is never considered for addition to any chains associated with that verb.

### 4.2 Schema Induction Procedure

In this section, we describe criteria for limiting schema growth based on a competition model among schemas for verbs. Chambers and Jurafsky (2009) descend the list of verbs ranked by their $narsim$ score, adding each new verb incrementally with $narsim(N, v_j) > \beta$—creating a new schema if $narsim(N, v_j) < \beta$—or before a hard limit of between six and twelve total events in a schema, a number that varies for different experimental purposes. Given that this algorithm is greedy, it is not entirely clear that it generates schemas that are globally optimal and best represent the narratives exhibited in the corpus.

Our aim is to avoid the creation of "low quality" schemas resulting from the addition of verbs that do not fit particularly well into one schema as compared to others. Yangarber (2003) provides a useful analogy in his description of *counter-training* in the discovery of patterns for information extraction. He notes that an "unsupervised algorithm does not know when to stop learning", so that "in the absence of a good stopping criterion, the resulting list of patterns must be manually reviewed". Yangarber's algorithm relies on competition among several different learners, each seeking patterns for a different "scenario" (a topic or domain). A pattern might have evidence favoring a learner to select it, but if learners for other scenarios also find evidence to acquire it, that counts against the first learners evidence.

The analogy that carries over to narrative schemas is that they reflect topics or domains, like Yangarber's scenarios. Narrative schemas are instantiated in individual documents, as sets of clauses. Thus, a particular clause should "belong to a single schema". On this analogy, we can formulate a version of counter-training by having each schema compete for the elements that constitute it. Those elements are verbs, which are thus the analogs of patterns. Their individual instantiations are clauses in documents – that is, a verb, its dependencies and their fillers. Clauses are thus the analogs to documents, because we wish to determine, for a given clause, which schema it instantiates, if any.

**Algorithm 1:** Counter-training for narrative event chain construction.

```
Data: Seed schemas, a scoring function
      scoring, pruning conditions
Result: narrative schemas
while number of SchemasGrowing and
Candidates both > 1 do
    initialize simtables S
    for every schema ∈ SchemasGrowing do
        initialize simtable s
        for every candidate ∈ Candidates do
            add
            scoring(schema, candidate) to
            s
        add s to S
    broadness[can] = Σ_{s∈S} Σ_{c∈s} 1
    for simtable in simtables do
        for can in broadness do
            simtable[can] −=
            broadness[can]
    induct highest-ranked Candidates into
    SchemasGrowing
    prune SchemasGrowing and
    Candidates
return GrownSchemas
```

Each schema ranks potential new additions in competition with other schemas. The specific process for this is detailed in Algorithm (1). In short, every candidate event is scored with respect to each schema and saved in $simtable$. Then the $broadness$—how well each candidate event scored with respect to all schemas—is computed. Each score is penalized based on the broadness, and the highest-ranked candidates are inducted into their respective schemas. The list of schemas and candidates are pruned according to the provided rules, and the process continues while there are both still candidates and schemas available.

Using a broadness table allows for schemas to compete with one another, and to do so irrespective of the order they are in. If many competing schemas rank a candidate event highly, they may only add it to themselves if the score outweighs the allotted penalties. If too many instances of a verb and its dependents seem to fit in different schemas, we drop it from the list of candidate additions to our narrative schemas. This does not preclude a verb belonging to two or more narrative schemas, since its individual occurrences might unmistakably belong to one schema or another, even after penalties have been deducted.

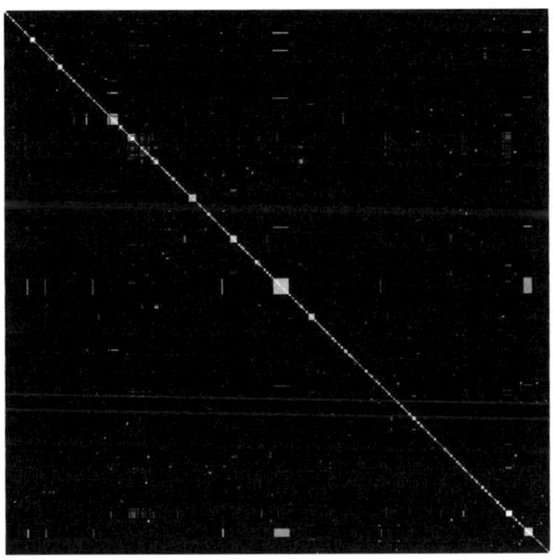

Figure 1: A grayscale confusion matrix showing overlap of events in schemas. Each column and row of pixels represents a schema, the schemas themselves arranged orthographically. Increasing brightness in a particular row and column indicates that more events overlap between the schemas represented by those respective rows and columns. Our counter-training algorithm is intended to produce schemas that are unique from others—that is, that follow the diagonal strongly.

Empirical evaluation with the cloze task is forthcoming. While we cannot enumerate all 800 of our schemas here,[2] Figure (2) and (3) show examples that indicate that our schemas are at least comparable with those others have extracted and are sufficient for looking at the interaction between schemas and document categories.

Our algorithm allows for the generation of duplicate schemas. Two schemas can easily converge if they were seeded with verbs that were closely related; once they include the same events, they are effectively identical. Figure (1) shows overlap between all 800 schemas.

[2]The full set can be found, in multiple formats, at: http://schemas.thedansimonson.com

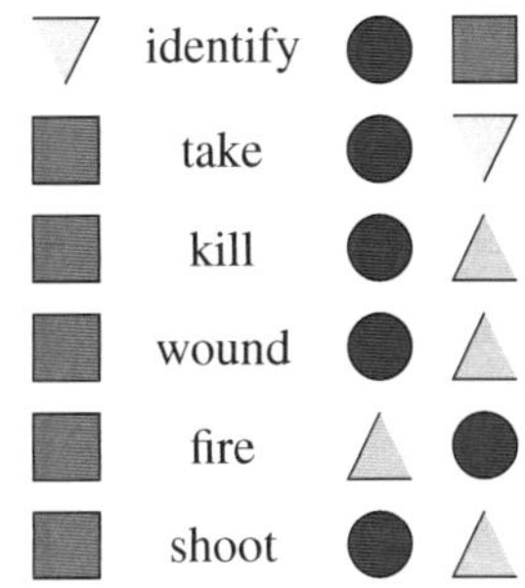


Figure 2: A schema extracted using our technique, generated for and used in the classification task. The red square and blue circle both indicate different PERSONs. The downward pointing yellow triangle indicates some THINGY; the upward pointing green triangle indicates either baghdad or a THINGY.

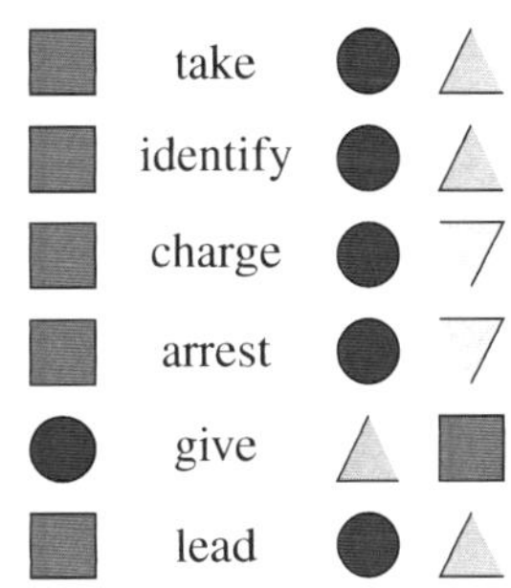


Figure 3: Another schema extracted using our technique, generated for and used in the classification task. Red squares are a police chain. Both blue circles and green, upward pointing triangles are independent PERSON chains. Downward pointing triangles are a chain referring to a killing.

## 5 Preparing Schemas for Classification Experiments

To better understand the properties of schemas, we will investigate how well schemas correlate with the document categories assigned within the NYT corpus. We will look at the schemas in two different ways—first, by assigning document categories to schemas, then by using these assignments to complete a categorization task. We do not expect the system to perform better than proven categorization techniques—rather, the categorization task acts as a proxy for investigating the distributional properties of schemas.

### 5.1 Retrieving Category Counts for Schemas

To employ schemas for classification, we will interpret them as a set of features. Effectively, if we think of the different event argument slots as nodes of a graph, the chains can be thought of as edges between nodes. These edges are pairs of verb dependency pairs which we will refer to as *co-referring argument pairs* (or CAPs, for short). To a great extent, CAPs preserve the information in the schema—the shared role fillers between events—while allowing for partial matches.

For example, Figure (2) contains a number of different chains. Some CAPs derived from this schema are $\{\langle \text{kill}, \texttt{SUBJ}\rangle, \langle \text{shoot}, \texttt{SUBJ}\rangle\}$ from the red square `PERSON` chain—derived, intuitively, from the fact that someone who shoots often kills—$\{\langle \text{fire}, \texttt{PREP}\rangle, \langle \text{shoot}, \texttt{OBJ}\rangle\}$ from the blue circle `PERSON` chain—derived from the fact that one may "shoot someone," but also "fire *at* someone"—among many, many others. This schema alone contains 37 CAPs: 15 each from the two chains that are shared in each and every role slot, and 7 from the other two auxiliary slots.

For a given set of chains $S^C$ from schema $S$, we disentangle the CAPs contained via the following:

$$\text{CAPs}(S) = \{\{vd_a, vd_b\} : \bigwedge_{x\in\{a,b\}} vd_x \in C \in S^C\} \tag{6}$$

where $C$ is a chain contained in the set of chains $S^C$, and $vd_x$ is any verb-dependency pair; $a$ and $b$ are arbitrary indices. We then can assign weights to a category $c$ for a schema $S$ by counting the categories of the documents that each CAP appears in, or more specifically:

$$W(c,S) = \sum_{d\in D} \begin{cases} w(c): & d \cap \text{CAPs}(S) \neq \emptyset \\ 0: & otherwise \end{cases} \tag{7}$$

where $D$ is the set of sets of CAPs from each of our training documents. $w(c)$ is a weighting function for a category. If we are working with simple document counts, $w_1(c) = 1$ is sufficient; alternatively, a cf-idf—like tf-idf but with categories instead of terms—could be used. This measure uses $w_{idf}(c) = \frac{N}{n_c}$, where $N$ is the total number of documents in the corpus and $n_c$ is the number of documents denoted as class $c$.

## 6 Classification Experiments

In order to understand the extent to which schematic information interacts with document categories, we considered individual, plausible components of schemas as baselines to compare against the performance of our full blown schema-based classifier. We discuss these in this section, as well as how the classification was performed, and how the target data set was chosen.

Each experiment represents a different way of extracting features from each schema. In other words, we still begin with schemas, but we extract the features between experiments. Each technique is intended as a plausible candidate for explaining how our schematic classifier works, working from the simplest to more complex collocations.

### 6.1 Experimental Models

In this section, we will discuss each of our baseline models, leading up to the features discussed in Section (5.1).

#### 6.1.1 Bag of Words Model

The bag of words model used here relies only on the presence of events found in our schemas for classification. Instead of thinking of each schema as a set of chains that are decomposed into CAPs, we look at each schema as a set of events $S^E$:

$$\mathbb{W}(S) = \{v_x : v_x \in S^E\} \tag{8}$$

where $v_x$ is a verb and $x$ is an arbitrary integer. The $\mathbb{W}$ of the schema in Figure (2) is $\{\texttt{shoot}, \texttt{fire}, \texttt{wound}, \texttt{kill}, \texttt{take}, \texttt{identify}\}$.

#### 6.1.2 Document Co-presence Model

In the document co-presence baseline model, if two events both appear in a document—regardless of their location or anything else—then that counts as an instance of that feature.

$$\mathbb{D}(S) = \{\{v_a, v_b\} : \bigwedge_{x\in\{a,b\}} v_x \in S^E\} \tag{9}$$

All permutations of pairs of events are considered. In a schema of size 6, this means that there are 15 pairs of events as features: $\{\{\texttt{shoot}, \texttt{fire}\}, \{\texttt{shoot}, \texttt{wound}\}, \dots$ *etc.*$\}$.

#### 6.1.3 Coreference Co-presence Model

Our final baseline creates pairs any two events which share co-referrent arguments. We do not include the specific argument slot. Now using $S^C$, the set of chains from schema $S$, instead of $S^E$:

$$\mathbb{C}(S) = \{\{v_a, v_b\} : \bigwedge_{x \in \{a,b\}} v_x \in S^C\} \quad (10)$$

This model's features are nearly schematic in nature, except that the features lack the specific slot wherein co-presence was defined; at this point, we effectively are using schemas without their role slot labels. Features derived from the schema in Figure (2) are no different from the last baseline because all events are shared with at least one chain. However, the interpretation of our hold-out documents changes. Because we are now looking at coreference, it is not the mere presence of a pair of events in the text, but their linkage through their arguments via coreference that counts.

#### 6.1.4 Schematic Classifier

This is our schematic classifier, as discussed above and illustrated with Equation (6). Note that Equation (10) is nearly identical to Equation (6); $v$ has been swapped with $vd$ representing the set of verb-dependency pairs. With verb-dependency pairs instead of verbs alone, we have built-up to a set of features that closely approximates our schemas.

### 6.2 Implementation

We used the `scikit-learn` class `sklearn.naive_bayes.MultinomialNB` to classify our documents (Pedregosa et al. 2011). Because our document categories overlap, we took a one-vs-all classification strategy for each document class; each document category represents a split into + or − classes. For the classification task, to give as much information as possible to the classifier, we generated 800 schemas seeded with the 800 most frequent verbs. We held-out $1/10^{th}$ of documents for evaluation.

In performing classification, we conducted a "rank descent." We started with the highest weighted category for a given feature in our first test, then used the two highest-weighted categories in the second experiment, etc., until every category that appeared with the feature is applied.

We completed the classification task in two separate sets of experiments using the raw counts weighting ($w_1$) in one and the cf-idf ($w_{idf}$) weighting scheme in the other.

## 7 Results

Table (1) contains a breakdown by category of peak performance. Categories that were better represented tend to have higher peak F1 scores. More poorly represented categories tended to peak in performance with the CAPs or at least coreference information provided by the coreference co-presence model $\mathbb{C}$, though this was not entirely the case—the very frequent category "crime" peaked with the $\mathbb{C}$.

Table 1: Number of documents per category retained from the "police" subset, along with the rank $n$ at which the rank descent reached the peak F1 value, which of the weighting functions $w_x$—$w_1$ or $w_{idf}$—was used from Section (5.1) and which of the models was used from Section (6.1) for which performance peaked with respect to F1. $\mathbb{W}$ is the bag of words model, $\mathbb{D}$ is document co-presence, $\mathbb{C}$ is coreference co-presence, and CAPs represents a fully schematic classifier. $N$ is the number of documents in a respective category. Some category names have been shortened or abbreviated.

| Category | $N$ | F1 | $n$ | $w_x$ | Model |
|---|---|---|---|---|---|
| Terrorism | 16,290 | 0.422 | 9 | *idf* | $\mathbb{W}$ |
| Crime | 14,685 | 0.461 | 6 | *idf* | $\mathbb{C}$ |
| Murders | 13,872 | 0.430 | 1 | 1 | $\mathbb{W}$ |
| World Trade Ctr. | 8,916 | 0.213 | 3 | 1 | CAPs |
| Violence | 6,450 | 0.183 | 5 | *idf* | $\mathbb{C}$ |
| Demonstr. and Riots | 6,430 | 0.193 | 4 | *idf* | $\mathbb{W}$ |
| Accidents | 5,719 | 0.166 | 4 | 1 | $\mathbb{W}$ |
| Police Brutality | 4,627 | 0.237 | 2 | 1 | $\mathbb{W}$ |
| Blacks | 3,522 | 0.166 | 6 | *idf* | $\mathbb{D}$ |
| Law and Legislation | 3,319 | 0.321 | 2 | 1 | $\mathbb{W}$ |
| Frauds | 1,848 | 0.136 | 7 | *idf* | $\mathbb{D}$ |
| Attacks on Police | 1,621 | 0.168 | 3 | 1 | $\mathbb{C}$ |
| Organized Crime | 871 | 0.098 | 4 | *idf* | $\mathbb{C}$ |
| Serial Murders | 918 | 0.075 | 8 | 1 | CAPs |
| Cocaine | 464 | 0.061 | 5 | *idf* | CAPs |
| Suburbs | 303 | 0.108 | 3 | *idf* | CAPs |
| Noise | 206 | 0.037 | 14 | 1 | $\mathbb{D}$ |
| Prison Escapes | 137 | 0.100 | 2 | *idf* | CAPs |

Figures (4) and (5) illustrate precision-recall curves for both series of *up to rank n* experiments. In all cases, $n$ goes up as we move from left to right; recall increases with each increase in $n$.

## 8 Discussion

Remarkably, we see some capability for schema-specific features to classify documents despite being generated without any explicit knowledge of the classifications they denote. Not in all cases is this the best, but it tends to help bolster performance in under-represented categories within the corpus. The precision-recall curves in Figures (4) and (5) illustrate our point—as we remove features

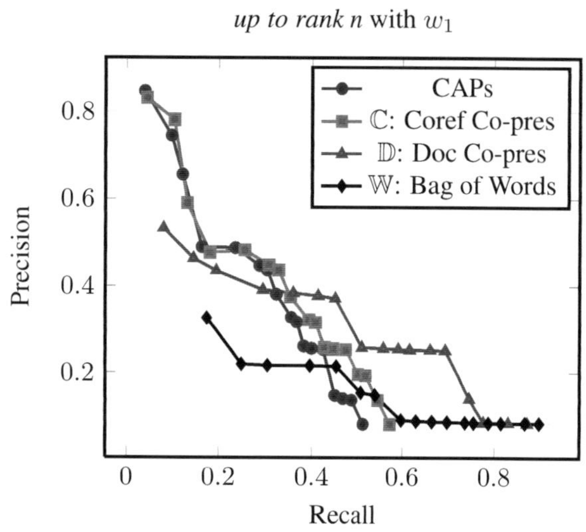


Figure 4: Precision/Recall curves for the *up to rank n* classification experiment using $w_1$ to assign categories to schemas.

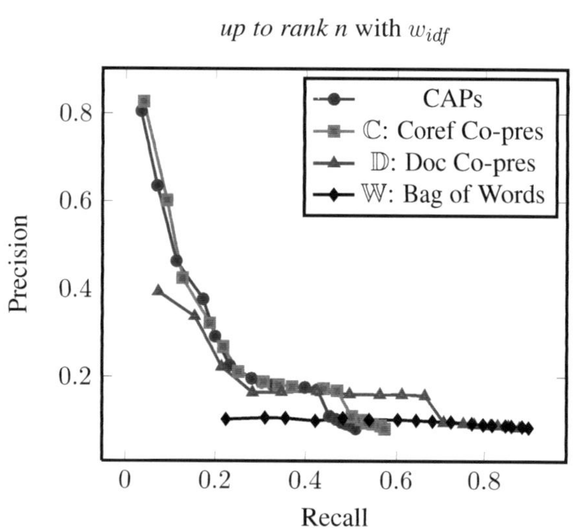


Figure 5: Precision/Recall curves for the *up to rank n* classification experiment using $w_{idf}$ to attach category assignments to schemas.

that our schemas uniquely provide, the peak precision generally declines. This shows that the features included in schemas do possess information specific to their associated document categories.

Of course, the rather simplified classifiers we've presented are by no means reflective of an industry standard classifier.[3] The number of features—only 6901 unique CAPs available, 1629 word types in the 𝕎 baseline—is less than what would be available to a typical bag of words analysis on the same data set—193702 word types. This performance produces precision-recall curves with a concave shape. However, what we do see is a suitable illustration that, with respect to the relationship between schemas and categories, the whole is greater than the sum of its parts.

Also worth noting is the fact that the precision-recall curve of the schematic classifier and the coreference co-presence classifier ℂ nearly adhere to one another. Figure (2) gives a great example of why slot information may not be helpful in all circumstances. In this schema, there are two very clear individuals in most of the events: a shooter of some sort, and someone who was shot. What about with *identify* and *take*? These are a bit more ambiguous; the precise utility of each exact argument slot is not as clear. The connections created through coreference, however, remain quite relevant and, alone, less error prone. This puts into question approaches that leave out coreference (Cheung, Poon, and Vandervende 2013; Balasubramanian et al., 2013)—with respect to this task, something was lost without it.

It is also necessary to critically question the efficacy of our source data, especially the largely unknown criteria used by the NYT Indexing Service to determine document categories. With respect to the schema in Figure (2), most individuals indubitably would say that such a schema is associated with murder. However, there are plenty of examples where *shooting*, *wounding*, and *killing* are not classified by the NYT Indexing Service as "Murders and Attempted Murders:"

> "A Brooklyn grand jury has cleared two police officers in the killing of an unarmed man whom they shot 18 times..."

[3]While our F1 scores across categories averaged 0.199, a non-schematic, bag-of-words Naïve Bayes classifier using all available word types averaged 0.458. Most categories outperformed the non-schematic classifier, except for Suburbs and Prison Escapes, which scored 0.000 with the non-schematic classifier.

> "The United States Marshal who shot and wounded a Queens high school student Thursday after mistaking the candy bar he was holding for a revolver..."

> "...the Police Department is being scrutinized over the shooting of several civilians by officers... a Hispanic teen-ager was shot in the back last month in Washington Heights."

In the words of Joe Strummer, "murder is a crime, unless it is done by a policeman." While we did not apply the types of role fillers explicitly to the classification task, these sorts of "errors" motivate the use of role fillers in future work.

## 9 Conclusions

We have shown techniques for deriving features from narrative schemas, and shown that features derived from narrative schemas are more than the sum of their parts. In particular, coreference information is a crucial component of them and seems—of the set of interpretations of schemas used—to produce the most substantial boost in precision.

## 10 Future Work

The long term goal of this work is to apply the information contained in narrative schemas to a real-world application. Knowing that schemas can act as precise identifiers of document categories improves our confidence in their usefulness. We hope to experiment with the use of additional features so that narrative schemas can serve as the basis for richer unsupervised knowledge extraction. We have discussed preliminary ideas for new ways to generate schemas as well, which we soon hope to evaluate.

## Acknowledgments

We'd like to thank the Georgetown Department of Linguistics for continued support, Amir Zeldes and Nate Chambers for feedback and discussions on components of this work, and the peer reviewers for insightful critiques.

## References

Balasubramanian, N., Soderland, S., Mausam, & Etzioni, O. 2013. Generating Coherent Event Schemas at Scale. In *EMNLP* (pp. 1721-1731).

Chambers, N., & Jurafsky, D. 2008. Unsupervised Learning of Narrative Event Chains. In *ACL* (pp. 789-797).

Chambers, N., & Jurafsky, D. 2009. Unsupervised learning of narrative schemas and their participants. *In Proceedings of the Joint Conference of the 47th Annual Meeting of the ACL and the 4th International Joint Conference on Natural Language Processing of the AFNLP: Volume 2-Volume 2* (pp. 602-610). Association for Computational Linguistics. Chicago

Chambers, N., & Jurafsky, D. 2011. Template-based information extraction without the templates. In *ACL-HLT 2011* (pp. 976-986). Association for Computational Linguistics.

Chambers, N. 2013. Event Schema Induction with a Probabilistic Entity-Driven Model. In *EMNLP* (pp. 1797-1807).

Cheung, J. C. K., Poon, H., & Vanderwende, L. 2013. Probabilistic frame induction. In *NAACL-HLT 2013* Association for Computational Linguistics.

Davidson, D. 1967. In Nicholas Rescher (ed.), *The Logic of Decision and Action*. University of Pittsburgh Press.

de Marneffe, M., MacCartney, B., and Manning, C.D. 2006. Generating Typed Dependency Parses from Phrase Structure Parses. In *LREC 2006*.

Finkel, J.R., Grenager, T., and Manning, C. 2005. Incorporating Non-local Information into Information Extraction Systems by Gibbs Sampling. In *ACL 2005* (pp. 363-370).

Jans, B., Bethard, S., Vuli, I., & Moens, M. F. 2012. Skip n-grams and ranking functions for predicting script events. In *EACL* (pp. 336-344). Association for Computational Linguistics.

Lee, H., Chang, A., Peirsman, Y., Chambers, N., Surdeanu, M., and Jurafsky, D. 2013. Deterministic coreference resolution based on entity-centric, precision-ranked rules. *Computational Linguistics* 39(4).

Manning, C. D., Surdeanu, M., Bauer, J., Finkel, J., Bethard, S. J., and McClosky, D. 2014. The Stanford CoreNLP Natural Language Processing Toolkit. In *ACL* (System Demonstrations, pp. 55-60).

Pedregosa, F., Varoquaux, G., Gramfort, A., Michel, V., Thirion, B., Grisel, O., ... & Duchesnay, E. 2011. Scikit-learn: Machine learning in Python. The Journal of Machine Learning Research, 12, (pp. 2825-2830).

Pichotta, K., & Mooney, R. J. 2014. Statistical Script Learning with Multi-Argument Events. In *EACL* (pp. 220-229).

Sandhaus, E. 2008. *The New York Times Annotated Corpus*. Linguistic Data Consortium, Philadelphia.

Schank, R.C. & Abelson, R.P. 1977. Scripts, plans, goals and understanding. Lawrence Erlbaum.

Yangarber, R. 2003. Counter-training in discovery of semantic patterns. In *ACL* (pp. 343-350). Association for Computational Linguistics.

# Improving Event Detection with Abstract Meaning Representation

**Xiang Li  Thien Huu Nguyen  Kai Cao  Ralph Grishman**
Computer Science Department
New York University
New York, NY 10003, USA
{xiangli,thien,kcao,grishman}@cs.nyu.edu

**Abstract**

Event Detection (ED) aims to identify instances of specified types of events in text, which is a crucial component in the overall task of event extraction. The commonly used features consist of lexical, syntactic, and entity information, but the knowledge encoded in the Abstract Meaning Representation (AMR) has not been utilized in this task. AMR is a semantic formalism in which the meaning of a sentence is encoded as a rooted, directed, acyclic graph. In this paper, we demonstrate the effectiveness of AMR to capture and represent the deeper semantic contexts of the trigger words in this task. Experimental results further show that adding AMR features on top of the traditional features can achieve 67.8% (with 2.1% absolute improvement) F-measure ($F_1$), which is comparable to the state-of-the-art approaches.

## 1 Introduction

The problem of event detection (ED) is identifying instances of specified types of events in text. Associated with each event mention, the event trigger (most often a single verb or nominalization) evokes that event. Our task, more precisely stated, involves identifying event triggers and classifying them into specific types. In this paper, we focus on the event detection task defined in Automatic Content Extraction (ACE) evaluation[1]. The task defines 8 event types and 33 subtypes such as *Die* and *End-Position*. For instance, according to the ACE 2005 annotation guideline, in the sentence "*A bomb* ***exploded*** *in central Baghdad yesterday*", an event detection system should be able to recognize the word "*exploded*" as a trigger for the event *Attack*. ED is a crucial component in the overall task of event extraction, which also involves event argument discovery[2]. This task is quite challenging, as the same event might appear with various trigger expressions, and an expression might also represent different events in different contexts.

Abstract Meaning Representation (AMR) (Dorr et al., 1998; Banarescu et al., 2013) (§2) is a semantic formalism in which the meaning of a sentence is encoded as a rooted, directed, acyclic graph. Nodes represent concepts, and labeled directed edges represent the relationships between them. The knowledge incorporated in the AMR (§3) can benefit the ED task by abstracting the semantic representation from the sentences with the same meaning but possibly in different syntactic forms. The results demonstrate that some characteristics are not completely captured by traditional features (e.g., dependency parse features), but may be revealed in the AMR, complementing other features to help boost the performance to 67.8% (with 2.1% absolute improvement) in $F_1$ (§4).

## 2 Abstract Meaning Representation

Abstract Meaning Representation (AMR) (Banarescu et al., 2013) is a sembanking language that captures whole sentence meanings in a rooted, directed, labeled, and (predominantly) acyclic graph structure - see Figure 1 for an example AMR parse. AMR utilizes multi-layer linguistic analysis such as PropBank frames, non-core semantic roles, coreference, named entity annotation, modality and negation to represent the semantic structure of a sentence. AMR strives for a more logical, less syntactic representation, collapsing some word category (verbs and nouns), word order, and morphological variation. Instead, it focuses on semantic relations between concepts and makes heavy use of predicate-argument structures as defined in PropBank (Kingsbury and Palmer,

[1] http://projects.ldc.upenn.edu/ace/

[2] Argument identification and argument role labeling are out of the scope of this paper, as planned for the future work.



*Proceedings of the First Workshop on Computing News Storylines*, pages 11–15,
Beijing, China, July 31, 2015. 

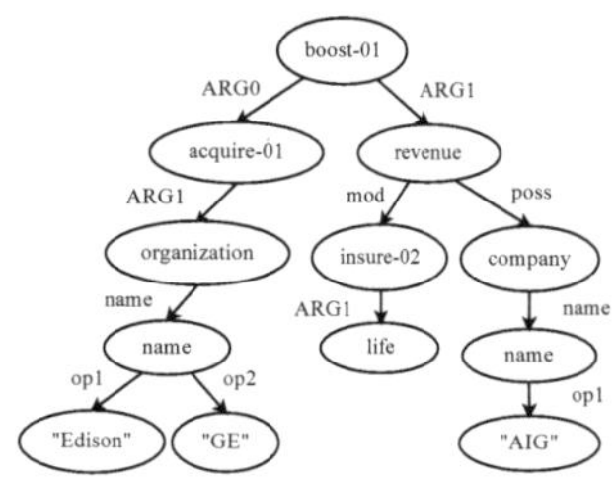


(a) AMR graph

```
(b / boost-01
  :ARG0 (a / acquire-01
    :ARG1 (o / organization
      :name (n2 / name
        :op1 "Edison"
        :op2 "GE")))
  :ARG1 (r / revenue
    :mod (i / insure-02
      :ARG1 (l / life))
    :poss (c / company
      :name (n / name
        :op1 "AIG"))))
```

(b) AMR annotation

Figure 1: Two equivalent ways of representing the AMR parse for the example sentence, "*The acquisition of Edison GE will boost AIG's annual life insurance revenue.*"

2002; Palmer et al., 2005). For example, a phrase like "*bond investor*" is represented using the frame "`invest-01`", even though no verbs appear.

In addition, many function words (determiners, prepositions) are considered to be syntactic "sugar" and are not explicitly represented in AMR, except for the semantic relations they signal. Hence, it assigns the same AMR parse graph to sentences that have the same basic meaning.[3]

Compared to traditional dependency parsing and semantic role labeling, the nodes in AMR are entities instead of words, and the edge types are much more fine-grained. AMR thus captures deeper meaning compared with other representations which are more commonly used to represent context in ED. In this work, all AMR parse graphs are automatically generated from the first published AMR parser, *JAMR* (Flanigan et al., 2014).

## 3 Framework and Features

To compare our proposed AMR features with the previous approaches, we implemented a Maximum Entropy (MaxEnt) classifier with both traditional features and AMR features for trigger identification and label classification.

[3]Readers can refer to (Banarescu et al., 2013) for a complete description of AMR and more examples.

To make a fair comparison, the feature sets in the baseline are identical to the local text features in (Li et al., 2013b). From Table 2, we can see that this baseline MaxEnt classifier with local features aligns well with the joint beam search approach using perceptron and local features in (Li et al., 2013b). The slight variation is mainly due to the different pre-processing procedures for features.

On top of the local features used in the baseline MaxEnt classifier, we exploit knowledge from AMR parse graphs to add AMR features into the MaxEnt classifier. The effects of these features have been explored based on the performance on the development dataset. More features have actually been studied, such as the features extracted from the grandparent node, the conjunction features of candidate and parent nodes, etc. Table 1 lists the final AMR features extracted from the AMR parse graph, and the corresponding feature values, for trigger candidate "*acquisition*", from the above example AMR graph.

## 4 Experiments

In this section, we will compare our MaxEnt classifiers using both baseline features and additional proposed AMR features with the state-of-the-art systems on the blind test set, and then discuss the results in more detail.

### 4.1 Dataset and Evaluation Metric

We evaluate our system with above presented features over the ACE 2005 corpus. For comparison purposes, we utilize the same test set with 40 newswire articles (672 sentences), the same development set with 30 other documents (836 sentences) and the same training set with the remaining 529 documents (14,849 sentences) as the previous studies on this dataset (Ji and Grishman, 2008; Liao and Grishman, 2010; Li et al., 2013b).

Following the previous work (Ji and Grishman, 2008; Liao and Grishman, 2010; Hong et al., 2011; Li et al., 2013b), a trigger candidate is counted as correct if its event subtype and offsets match those of a reference trigger. The ACE 2005 corpus has 33 event subtypes that, along with one class "*Other*" for the non-trigger tokens, constitutes a 34-class classification problem in this work. Finally we use *Precision (P)*, *Recall (R)*, and *F-measure ($F_1$)* to evaluate the performance. Table 2 presents the overall performance of the systems with gold-standard entity mention and

| Node | Feature | Description | Example |
|---|---|---|---|
| Candidate | amr_word_tag | The conjunction of the candidate word and its AMR tag | `acquire-01_ARG0` |
| Root | amr_dist_to_root | The distance between the candidate word and the root | `1` |
| Parent | amr_parent_word | The word of the parent node | `boost-01` |
| | amr_parent_tag | The AMR tag of the parent node | `AMR-Root` |
| | amr_parent_word_tag | The conjunction of the parent word and its AMR tag | `boost-01_AMR-Root` |
| Sibling | amr_sibling_tag | The AMR tag of each sibling node | `ARG1` |
| | amr_sibling_word_tag | The conjunction of the sibling word and its AMR tag | `revenue_ARG1` |
| Children | amr_child_word_tag | The conjunction of the child word and its AMR tag | `organization_ARG1` |
| Grandchildren | amr_grandchild_word | The word of the grandchild node | `name` |

Table 1: Features extracted from the AMR graph and example features for candidate "*acquisition*".

| Methods | $P$ | $R$ | $F_1$ |
|---|---|---|---|
| Sentence-level in Hong et al. (2011) | 67.6 | 53.5 | 59.7 |
| MaxEnt classifier with local features in Li et al. (2013b) | 74.5 | 59.1 | 65.9 |
| Joint beam search with local features in Li et al. (2013b) | 73.7 | 59.3 | 65.7 |
| Joint beam search with local and global features in Li et al. (2013b) | 73.7 | 62.3 | 67.5 |
| Cross-entity in Hong et al. (2011) † | 72.9 | 64.3 | 68.3 |
| MaxEnt classifier with baseline features | 70.8 | 61.4 | 65.7 |
| MaxEnt classifier with baseline + AMR features | 74.4 | 62.3 | **67.8** |

Table 2: Performance (%) comparison with the state-of-the-art systems. † beyond sentence level.

type information[4].

As we can see from Table 2, among the systems that only use sentence level information, our MaxEnt classifier using both baseline and AMR features significantly outperforms the MaxEnt classifier with baseline features as well as the joint beam search with local features from Li et al. (2013b) (an absolute improvement of 2.1% in $F_1$ score), and performs comparably (67.8% in $F_1$) to the state-of-the-art joint beam search approach using both local and global features (67.5% in $F_1$) (Li et al., 2013b). This is remarkable since our MaxEnt classifier does not require any global features[5] or sophisticated machine learning framework with a much larger hypothesis space, e.g., structured perceptron with beam search (Li et al., 2013b).

From the detailed result analysis, we can see that the event trigger detection of most event types are significantly ($p < 0.05$) improved over the baseline setting. Many types gain substantially in both precision and recall, while only 4 out of 33 event types decrease slightly in performance. Table 3 presents the performance comparison for a subset of event types between the baseline and the classifier with both baseline and AMR features[6].

For instance, in the test sentence "*... have Scud missiles capable of* ***reaching*** *Israel ...*", the trigger candidate "*reach*" can be a *Conflict:Attack* event (as in this case) but also a *Contact:Phone-Write* event (e.g., "*they tried to reach their loved ones*"). If the subject (`ARG0`) is a weapon (as in this example), it should be an *Attack* event. This pattern can be learned from a sentence such as "*The missiles ... reach their target*". The AMR parser is able to look through "*capable of*" and recognizes that "*missiles*" is the subject (`:ARG0 m2/missile`) of "*reach*" in this example. Thus AMR features are able to help predict the correct event type in this case.

AMR can also analyze and learn from different forms of the same word. For example, there are two examples in the ACE corpus involving "*repay*", one using the verb ("*repaying*") and the other one using the noun ("*repayment*"), and both are classified as *Transaction:Transfer-money* event. AMR could learn from the "*repaying*" example about the correct event type and then precisely apply it to the "*repayment*" example.

The gains from adding AMR features show that the features and knowledge encoded in the AMR parse graphs can complement the information incorporated in the dependency parse trees and other traditional features.

[4]Entity mentions and types may get used to introduce more features into the systems.

[5]Global features are the features generated from several event trigger candidates, such as bigrams of trigger types which occur in the same sentence or the same clause, binary feature indicating whether synonyms in the same sentence have the same trigger label, context and dependency paths between two triggers conjuncted with their types, etc.

[6]Because of the limited space, only a subset of event types is listed in Table 3.

| Event Type | Baseline | | | Baseline + AMR | | |
|---|---|---|---|---|---|---|
| | $P$ | $R$ | $F_1$ | $P$ | $R$ | $F_1$ |
| Transaction:Transfer-Ownership | 50.0 | 11.1 | 18.2 | 62.5 | 18.5 | 28.6 |
| Business:Start-Org | 0.0 | 0.0 | 0.0 | 100.0 | 5.9 | 11.1 |
| Justice:Trial-Hearing | 80.0 | 80.0 | 80.0 | 83.3 | 100.0 | 90.9 |
| Justice:Appeal | 85.7 | 100.0 | 92.3 | 100.0 | 100.0 | 100.0 |
| Conflict:Demonstrate | 80.0 | 57.1 | 66.7 | 100.0 | 57.1 | 72.8 |
| Justice:Arrest-Jail | 75.0 | 50.0 | 60.0 | 83.3 | 83.3 | 83.3 |
| Contact:Phone-Write | 20.0 | 12.5 | 15.4 | 40.0 | 25.0 | 30.8 |
| Personnel:Start-Position | 80.0 | 33.3 | 47.1 | 66.7 | 33.3 | 44.4 |
| Justice:Release-Parole | 50.0 | 100.0 | 66.7 | 33.3 | 100.0 | 50.0 |
| Contact:Meet | 85.7 | 87.1 | 86.4 | 82.3 | 82.3 | 82.3 |

Table 3: Comparison between the performance (%) of baseline and AMR on a subset of event types.

### 4.2 Discussion

Applying the AMR features separately, we find that the features extracted from the sibling nodes are the best predictors of correctness, which indicates that the contexts of sibling nodes associated with the AMR tags can provide better evidence for word sense disambiguation of the trigger candidate as needed for event type classification. Features from the parent node and children nodes are also significant contributors.

Performance of the current AMR parser suffers from a lack of training data. For example,

1. *A tank **fired** on the Palestine Hotel.*
2. *The company **fired** its president.*

where two "*fired*" are assigned the same PropBank frame (a very coarse notion of word sense), "`fire-01`", rather than distinguishing the different senses here. As measured in the *JAMR* description paper (Flanigan et al., 2014), this parser only achieves 58% in $F_1$ on the test data using the full pipeline (concept identification and relation identification stages). An AMR parser trained on a larger corpus would help much more on this ED task and other Information Extraction tasks.

## 5 Related Work

Early research on event detection has primarily focused on local sentence-level representation of trigger candidates in a pipeline architecture (Grishman et al., 2005; Ahn, 2006). Meanwhile, higher level features have been investigated to improve the performance, including: Ji and Grishman (2008); Gupta and Ji (2009); Patwardhan and Riloff (2009); Liao and Grishman (2010; 2011); Hong et al. (2011); McClosky et al. (2011); Huang and Riloff (2012); Li et al. (2012), and Li et al. (2013a). Besides, some recent research has worked on joint models, including methods based on Markov Logic Networks (Riedel et al., 2009; Poon and Vanderwende, 2010; Venugopal et al., 2014), structured perceptrons (Li et al., 2013b), and dual decomposition (Riedel and McCallum (2009; 2011a; 2011b)). However, all of these methods as mentioned above have not exploited the knowledge captured in the AMR.

A growing number of researchers are studying how to incorporate the knowledge encoded in the AMR parse and representations to help solve other NLP problems, such as entity linking (Pan et al., 2015), machine translation (Jones et al., 2015), and summarization (Liu et al., 2015). Especially the appearance of the first published AMR parser (Flanigan et al., 2014) will benefit and spur a lot of new research conducted using AMR.

## 6 Conclusion and Future Work

Event Detection requires a representation of the relations between the event trigger word and entities in text. We demonstrate that Abstract Meaning Representation can capture deeper contexts of trigger words in this task, and the experimental results show that adding AMR features on top of the traditional features can achieve 67.8% in F-measure with 2.1% absolute improvement over the baseline features. We show that AMR enables ED performance to become comparable to the state-of-the-art approaches.

In this work, we have only applied a subset of AMR representations to the ED task, so we aim to explore more AMR knowledge to be utilized in this task and other Information Extraction tasks, e.g., event argument identification and argument role classification. Furthermore, we are also interested in using AMR knowledge in different machine learning frameworks, such as incorporating the AMR into the SVM tree kernel.

## References


David Ahn. 2006. The stages of event extraction. In *Proceedings of the Workshop on Annotating and Reasoning About Time and Events*, pages 1–8.

Laura Banarescu, Claire Bonial, Shu Cai, Madalina Georgescu, Kira Griffitt, Ulf Hermjakob, Kevin Knight, Philipp Koehn, Martha Palmer, and Nathan Schneider. 2013. Abstract meaning representation for sembanking. In *Proceedings of ACL 2013 Workshop on Linguistic Annotation and Interoperability with Discourse*.

Bonnie Dorr, Nizar Habash, and David Traum. 1998. A thematic hierarchy for efficient generation from lexical-conceptual structure. In *Proceedings of the Third Conference of the Association for Machine Translation in the Americas, AMTA-98, in Lecture Notes in Artificial Intelligence*, pages 333–343.

Jeffrey Flanigan, Sam Thomson, Jaime G. Carbonell, Chris Dyer, and Noah A. Smith. 2014. A discriminative graph-based parser for the abstract meaning representation. In *Proceedings of ACL*, pages 1426–1436.

Ralph Grishman, David Westbrook, and Adam Meyers. 2005. NYU's english ACE 2005 system description. In *ACE 2005 Evaluation Workshop*.

Prashant Gupta and Heng Ji. 2009. Predicting unknown time arguments based on cross-event propagation. In *Proceedings of ACL-IJCNLP*, pages 369–372.

Yu Hong, Jianfeng Zhang, Bin Ma, Jian-Min Yao, Guodong Zhou, and Qiaoming Zhu. 2011. Using cross-entity inference to improve event extraction. In *Proceedings of ACL*, pages 1127–1136.

Ruihong Huang and Ellen Riloff. 2012. Modeling textual cohesion for event extraction. In *Proceedings of AAAI*.

Heng Ji and Ralph Grishman. 2008. Refining event extraction through cross-document inference. In *Proceedings of ACL*, pages 254–262.

Bevan Jones, Jacob Andreas, Daniel Bauer, Karl Moritz Hermann, and Kevin Knight. 2015. Semantics-based machine translation with hyperedge replacement grammars. In *Proceedings of COLING*.

Paul Kingsbury and Martha Palmer. 2002. From treebank to propbank. In *Proceedings of LREC*.

Peifeng Li, Guodong Zhou, Qiaoming Zhu, and Libin Hou. 2012. Employing compositional semantics and discourse consistency in chinese event extraction. In *Proceedings of EMNLP*, pages 1006–1016.

Peifeng Li, Qiaoming Zhu, and Guodong Zhou. 2013a. Argument inference from relevant event mentions in chinese argument extraction. In *Proceedings of ACL*, pages 1477–1487.

Qi Li, Heng Ji, and Liang Huang. 2013b. Joint event extraction via structured prediction with global features. In *Proceedings of ACL*, pages 73–82.

Shasha Liao and Ralph Grishman. 2010. Using document level cross-event inference to improve event extraction. In *Proceedings of ACL*, pages 789–797.

Shasha Liao and Ralph Grishman. 2011. Acquiring topic features to improve event extraction: in preselected and balanced collections. In *Proceedings of RANLP*, pages 9–16.

Fei Liu, Jeffrey Flanigan, Sam Thomson, Norman Sadeh, and Noah A. Smith. 2015. Toward abstractive summarization using semantic representations. In *Proceedings of NAACL*.

David McClosky, Mihai Surdeanu, and Chris Manning. 2011. Event extraction as dependency parsing. In *Proceedings of ACL*, pages 1626–1635.

Martha Palmer, Paul Kingsbury, and Daniel Gildea. 2005. The proposition bank: An annotated corpus of semantic roles. *Computational Linguistics*, 31.

Xiaoman Pan, Taylor Cassidy, Ulf Hermjakob, Heng Ji, and Kevin Knight. 2015. Unsupervised entity linking with abstract meaning representation. In *Proceedings of NAACL-HLT*.

Siddharth Patwardhan and Ellen Rilof. 2009. A unified model of phrasal and sentential evidence for information extraction. In *Proceedings of EMNLP*, pages 151–160.

Hoifung Poon and Lucy Vanderwende. 2010. Joint inference for knowledge extraction from biomedical literature. In *Proceedings of NAACL*, pages 813–821.

Sebastian Riedel and Andrew McCallum. 2011a. Fast and robust joint models for biomedical event extraction. In *Proceedings of EMNLP*, pages 1–12.

Sebastian Riedel and Andrew McCallum. 2011b. Robust biomedical event extraction with dual decomposition and minimal domain adaptation. In *Proceedings of the BioNLP Shared Task 2011 Workshop*, pages 46–50.

Sebastian Riedel, Hong-Woo Chun, Toshihisa Takagi, and Jun'ichi Tsujii. 2009. A markov logic approach to bio-molecular event extraction. In *Proceedings of the BioNLP 2009 Workshop Companion Volume for Shared Task*, pages 41–49.

Deepak Venugopal, Chen Chen, Vibhav Gogate, and Vincent Ng. 2014. In *Proceddings of EMNLP*.

# News clustering approach based on discourse text structure

**Tatyana Makhalova**
National Research University
Higher School of Economics
Moscow, Russia
t.makhalova@gmail.com

**Dmitry Ilvovsky**
National Research University
Higher School of Economics
Moscow, Russia
dilvovsky@hse.ru

**Boris Galitsky**
Knowledge Trail Incorporated
San Jose, USA
bgalitsky@hotmail.com

## Abstract

A web search engine usually returns a long list of documents and it may be difficult for users to navigate through this collection and find the most relevant ones. We present an approach to post-retrieval snippet clustering based on pattern structures construction on augmented syntactic parse trees. Since an algorithm may be too slow for a typical collection of snippets, we propose a reduction method that allows us to construct a reduced pattern structure and make it scalable. Our algorithm takes into account discourse information to make clustering results independent of how information is distributed between sentences.

## 1 Introduction and related works

The document clustering problem was widely investigated in many applications of text mining. One of the most important aspects of the text clustering problem is a structural representation of texts. A common approach to the text representation is a vector space model (Salton et al., 1975), where the collection or corpus of documents is represented as a term-document matrix. The main drawback of this model is its inability to reflect the importance of a word with respect to a document and a corpus. To tackle this issue the weighted scheme based on tf-idf score has been proposed. Also, a term-document matrix built on a large texts collection may be sparse and have a high dimensionality. To reduce feature space, PCA, truncated SVD (Latent Semantic Analysis), random projection and other methods have been proposed. To handle synonyms as similar terms the general Vector Space Model (Wong et al., 1985; Tsatsaronis and Panagiotopoulou, 2009), topic-based vector model (Becker and Kuropka, 2003) and enhanced topic-based vector space model (Polyvyanyy and Kuropka, 2007) were introduced. The most common ways to clustering term-document matrix are hierarchical clustering, k-means and also bisecting k-means.

Graph models are also used for text representation. Document Index Graph (DIG) was proposed by Hammouda (2004). Zamir and Etzioni (1998) use suffix tree for representing web snippets, where words are used instead of characters. A more sophisticated model based on n-grams was introduced in Schenker et al. (2007).

In this paper, we consider a particular application of document clustering, it is a representation of web search results that could improve navigation through relevant documents. Clustering snippets on salient phrases is described in (Zamir and Etzioni, 1999; Zeng et al., 2004). But the most promising approach for document clustering is a conceptual clustering, because it allows to obtain overlapping clusters and to organize them into a hierarchical structure as well (Cole et al., 2003; Koester, 2006; Messai et al., 2008; Carpineto and Romano, 1996). We present an approach to selecting most significant clusters based on a pattern structure (Ganter and Kuznetsov, 2001). An approach of extended representation of syntactic trees with discourse relations between them was introduced in (Galitsky et al., 2013). Leveraging discourse information allows to combine news articles not only by keyword similarity but by broader topicality and writing styles as well.

The paper is organized as follows. Section 2 introduces a parse thicket and its simplified representation. In section 3 we consider approach to clustering web snippets and discuss efficiency issues. The illustrative example is presented in section 4. Finally, we conclude the paper and discuss some research perspectives.



*Proceedings of the First Workshop on Computing News Storylines*, pages 16–20,
Beijing, China, July 31, 2015. 

## 2 Clustering based on pattern structure

**Parse Thickets** Parse thicket (Galitsky et al., 2013) is defined as a set of parse trees for each sentence augmented with a number of arcs, reflecting inter-sentence relations. In present work we use parse thickets based on limited set of relations described in (Galitsky et al., 2013): coreferences (Lee et al., 2012), Rhetoric structure relations (Mann and Thompson, 1992) and Communicative Actions (Searle, 1969).

**Pattern Structure with Parse Thickets simplification** To apply parse thickets to text clustering tasks we use pattern structures (Ganter and Kuznetsov, 2001) that is defined as a triple $(G, (D, \sqcap), \delta)$, where $G$ is a set of objects, $(D, \sqcap)$ is a complete meet-semilattice of descriptions and $\delta : G \to D$ is a mapping an object to a description. The Galois connection between set of objects and their descriptions is also defined as follows:

$$A^{\diamond} := g \in A \prod \delta(g)$$

$$d^{\diamond} := \{g \in G | d \sqsubseteq \delta(g)\}$$

for $A \subseteq G$, for $d \in D$

A pair $\langle A, d \rangle$ for which $A^{\diamond} = d$ and $d^{\diamond} = A$ is called a pattern concept. In our case, $A$ is the set of news, $d$ is their shared content.

We use AddIntent algorithm (van der Merwe et al., 2004) to construct pattern structure. On each step, it takes the parse thicket (or chunks) of a web snippet of the input and plugs it into the pattern structure.

A pattern structure has several drawbacks. Firstly, the size of the structure could grow exponentially on the input data. More than that, construction of a pattern structure could be computationally intensive. To address the performance issues, we reduce the set of all intersections between the members of our training set (maximal common sub-parse thickets).

## 3 Reduced pattern structure

Pattern structure constructed from a collection of short texts usually has a huge number of concepts. To reduce the computational costs and improve the interpretability of pattern concepts we introduce several metrics, that are described below.

**Average and Maximal Pattern Score** The average and maximal pattern score indices are meant to assess how meaningful the common description of texts in the concept is. The higher the difference of text fragments from each other, the lower their shared content is. Thus, meaningfulness criterion of the group of texts is

$$Score^{max} \langle A, d \rangle := max_{chunk \in d} Score(chunk)$$

$$Score^{avg} \langle A, d \rangle := \frac{1}{|d|} \sum_{chunk \in d} Score(chunk)$$

The score function $Score(chunk)$ estimates chunks on the basis of parts of speech composition.

**Average and Minimal Pattern Score loss** Average and minimal pattern score loss describe how much information contained in text is lost in the description with respect to the source texts. Average pattern score loss expresses the average loss of shared content for all texts in a concept, while minimal pattern score loss represents a minimal loss of content among all texts included in a concept.

$$ScoreLoss^{min} \langle A, d \rangle := \min_{g \in A} Score^{max} \langle g, d_g \rangle$$

$$ScoreLoss^{avg} \langle A, d \rangle := \frac{1}{|d|} \sum_{g \in A} Score^{max} \langle g, d_g \rangle$$

We propose to use a reduced pattern structure. There are two options in our approach. The first one - construction of lower semilattice. This is similar to iceberg concept lattice approach (Stumme et al., 2002). The second option - construction of concepts which are different from each other. Thus, for arbitrary sets of texts $A_1$ and $A_2$, corresponding descriptions $d_1$ and $d_2$ and candidate for a pattern concept $\langle A_1 \cup A_2, d_1 \cap d_2 \rangle$ criterion has the following form

$$Score^{max} \langle A_1 \cup A_2, d_1 \cap d_2 \rangle \geq \theta$$

$$Score^{*} \langle A_1 \cup A_2, d_1 \cap d_2 \rangle \geq \mu_1 min \{Score^{*} \langle A_1, d_1 \rangle, Score^{*} \langle A_2, d_2 \rangle\}$$

$$Score^{*} \langle A_1 \cup A_2, d_1 \cap d_2 \rangle \leq \mu_2 max \{Score^{*} \langle A_1, d_1 \rangle, Score^{*} \langle A_2, d_2 \rangle\}$$

The first constraint provides the condition for the construction of concepts with meaningful content, while two other constrains ensure that we do not use concepts with similar content.

## 4 Experiments

In this section we consider the proposed clustering method on 2 examples. The first one corresponds to the case when clusters are overlapping and distinguishable, the second one is the case of non-overlapping clusters.

### 4.1 User Study

In some cases it is quite difficult to identify disjoint classes for a text collection. To confirm this, we conducted experiments similar to the experiment scheme described in (Zeng et al., 2004). We took web snippets obtained by querying the Bing search engine API and asked a group of four assessors to label ground truth for them. We performed news queries related to world's most pressing news (for example, "fighting Ebola with nanoparticles", "turning brown eyes blue", "F1 winners", "read facial expressions through webcam", "2015 ACM awards winners") to make labeling of data easier for the assessors.

In most cases, according to the assessors, it was difficult to determine partitions, while overlapping clusters naturally stood out. As a result, in the case of non-overlapping clusters we usually got a small number of large classes or a sufficiently large number of classes consisting of 1-2 snippets. More than that, for the same set of snippets we obtained quite different partitions.

We used the Adjusted Mutual Information score to estimate pairwise agreement of non-overlapping clusters, which were identified by the people.

To demonstrate the failure of the conventional clustering approach we consider 12 short texts on news query "The Ebola epidemic". Tests are available by link [1].

Assessors identify quite different non-overlapping clusters. The pairwise Adjusted Mutual Information score was in the range of 0,03 to 0,51. Next, we compared partitions to clustering results of the following clustering methods: k-means clustering based on vectors obtained by truncated SVD (retaining at least 80% of the information), hierarchical agglomerative clustering (HAC), complete and average linkage of the term-document matrix with Manhattan distance and cosine similarity, hierarchical agglomerative clustering (both linkage) of tf-idf matrix with Euclidean metric. In other words, we turned an unsupervised learning problem into the supervised one. The accuracy score for different clustering methods is represented in Figure 1. Curves correspond to the different partitions that have been identified by people.

As it was mentioned earlier, we obtain inconsistent "true" labeling. Thereby the accuracy of clustering differs from labeling made by evaluators. This approach doesn't allow to determine the best partition, because a partition itself is not natural for the given news set. For example, consider clusters obtained by HAC based on cosine similarity (trade-off between high accuracy and its low variation):

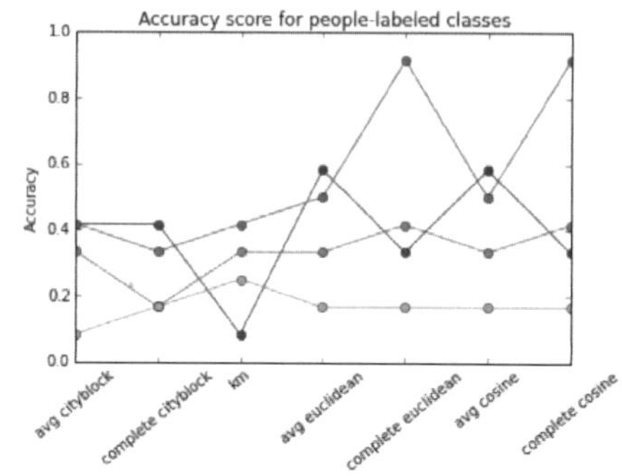


Figure 1: Classification accuracy of clustering results and "true" clustering (example 1). Four lines are different news labeling made by people. The y-axis values for fixed x-value correspond to classification accuracy of a clustering method for each of the four labeling

1-st cluster: 1,2,7,9;

2-nd cluster: 3,11,12;

3-rd cluster: 4,8;

4-th cluster: 5,6;

5-th cluster: 10.

Almost the same news 4, 8, 12 and 9, 10 are in the different clusters. News 10, 11 should be simultaneously in several clusters (1-st, 5-th and 2-nd,3-rd respectively).

### 4.2 Examples of pattern structures clustering

To construct hierarchy of overlapping clusters by the proposed methods, we use the following constraints: $\theta = 0,25$, $\mu_1 = 0,1$ and $\mu_2 = 0,9$. The value of $\theta$ limits the depth of the pattern structure (the maximal number of texts in a cluster), put differently, the higher $\theta$, the closer should be the general intent of clusters. $\mu_1$ and $\mu_2$ determine the degree of dissimilarity of the clusters on different levels of the lattice (the clusters are prepared by adding a new document to the current one).

We consider the proposed clustering method on 2 examples. The first one was described above, it corresponds to the case of overlapping clusters, the second one is the case when clusters are non-overlapping and distinguishable. Texts of the sec-

[1] https://github.com/anonymously1/CNS2015/blob/master/NewsSet1

ond example are available by link [2]. Three clusters are naturally identified in this texts.

The cluster distribution depending on volume are shown in Table 1. We got 107 and 29 clusters for the first and the second example respectively.

| Text number | Clusters number | |
|---|---|---|
| | Example 1 | Example 2 |
| 1 | 12 | 11 |
| 2 | 34 | 15 |
| 3 | 33 | 3 |
| 4 | 20 | 0 |
| 5 | 7 | 0 |
| 6 | 1 | 0 |

Table 1: The clusters volume distribution for non-overlapping clusters (example 1) and overlapping clusters (example 2)

In fact, this method is an agglomerative hierarchical clustering with overlapping clusters. Hierarchical structure of clusters provides browsing of texts with similar content by layers. The cluster structure is represented on Figure 2. The top of the structure corresponds to meaningless clusters that consist of all texts. Upper layer consists of clusters with large volume.

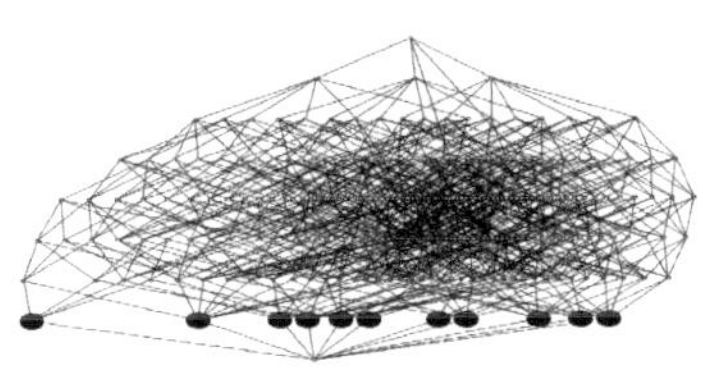

(a) pattern structure without reduction

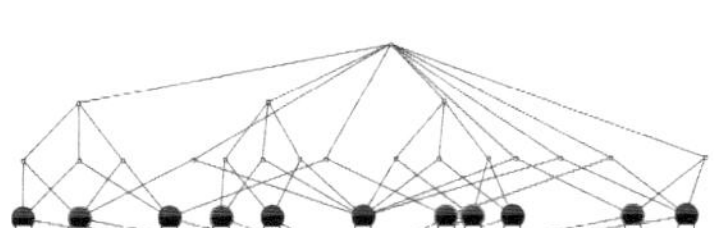

(b) reduced pattern structure

Figure 2: The cluster structure (example 2). The node on the top corresponds to the "dummy" cluster, high level nodes correspond to the big clusters with quite general content, while the clusters at lower levels correspond to more specific news.

Clustering based on pattern structures provides well interpretable groups.

The upper level of hierarchy (the most representative clusters for example 1) consists of the clusters presented in Table 2.

[2]https://github.com/anonymously1/CNS2015/blob/master/NewsSet

| MaxScore | Cluster (extent) |
|---|---|
| 3,8 | { 1, 2, 3, 5, 7, 9 } |
| 2,4 | { 1, 2, 6, 9, 10 } |
| 3,8 | { 1, 5, 11 } |
| 2,3 | { 1, 5, 6 } |
| 3,3 | { 2, 4, 11 } |
| 7,8 | { 3, 11, 12} |
| 3,2 | { 3, 9, 11 } |
| 4,1 | { 4, 8, 11 } |
| 3,8 | { 1, 11 } |
| 3,3 | { 2, 11 } |
| 2,8 | { 3, 10 } |
| 3,3 | { 5, 6 } |

Table 2: Scores of representative clusters

We also consider smaller clusters and select those for which adding of any object (text) dramatically reduces the $MaxScore$ $\{1, 2, 3, 7, 9\}$ and $\{5, 6\}$. For other nested clusters significant decrease of $MaxScore$ occurred exactly with the an expansion of single clusters.

For the second example we obtained 3 clusters that corresponds to "true" labeling.

Our experiments show that pattern structure clustering allows to identify easily interpretable groups of texts and significantly improves text browsing.

## 5 Conclusion

In this paper, we presented an approach that addressed the problem of short text clustering. Our study shows a failure of the traditional clustering methods, such as k-means and HAC. We propose to use parse thickets that retain the structure of sentences instead of the term-document matrix and to build the reduced pattern structures to obtain overlapping groups of texts. Experimental results demonstrate considerable improvement of browsing and navigation through texts set for users. Introduced indices $Score$ and $ScoreLoss$ both improve computing efficiency and tackle the problem of redundant clusters.

An important direction for future work is to take into account synonymy and to compare the proposed method to similar approach that use key words instead of parse thickets.

## References


Jörg Becker and Dominik Kuropka. 2003. Topic-based vector space model. In *Proceedings of the 6th International Conference on Business Information Systems*, pages 7–12.

Claudio Carpineto and Giovanni Romano. 1996. A lattice conceptual clustering system and its application to browsing retrieval. *Machine learning*, 24(2):95–122.

Richard Cole, Peter Eklund, and Gerd Stumme. 2003. Document retrieval for e-mail search and discovery using formal concept analysis. *Applied artificial intelligence*, 17(3):257–280.

Boris Galitsky, Dmitry Ilvovsky, Sergey Kuznetsov, and Fedor Strok. 2013. Matching sets of parse trees for answering multi-sentence questions. *Proc. Recent Advances in Natural Language Processing (RANLP 2013), Bulgaria*.

Bernhard Ganter and Sergei O Kuznetsov. 2001. Pattern structures and their projections. In *Conceptual Structures: Broadening the Base*, pages 129–142. Springer.

Khaled M Hammouda and Mohamed S Kamel. 2004. Document similarity using a phrase indexing graph model. *Knowledge and Information Systems*, 6(6):710–727.

Bjoern Koester. 2006. Conceptual knowledge retrieval with fooca: Improving web search engine results with contexts and concept hierarchies. In *Advances in Data Mining. Applications in Medicine, Web Mining, Marketing, Image and Signal Mining*, pages 176–190. Springer.

Heeyoung Lee, Marta Recasens, Angel Chang, Mihai Surdeanu, and Dan Jurafsky. 2012. Joint entity and event coreference resolution across documents. In *Proceedings of the 2012 Joint Conference on Empirical Methods in Natural Language Processing and Computational Natural Language Learning*, pages 489–500. Association for Computational Linguistics.

William C Mann and Sandra A Thompson. 1992. *Discourse description: Diverse linguistic analyses of a fund-raising text*, volume 16. John Benjamins Publishing.

Nizar Messai, Marie-Dominique Devignes, Amedeo Napoli, and Malika Smail-Tabbone. 2008. Many-valued concept lattices for conceptual clustering and information retrieval. In *ECAI*, volume 178, pages 127–131.

Artem Polyvyanyy and Dominik Kuropka. 2007. A quantitative evaluation of the enhanced topic-based vector space model.

Gerard Salton, Anita Wong, and Chung-Shu Yang. 1975. A vector space model for automatic indexing. *Communications of the ACM*, 18(11):613–620.

Adam Schenker, Horst Bunke, Mark Last, and Abraham Kandel. 2007. Clustering of web documents using graph representations. In *Applied Graph Theory in Computer Vision and Pattern Recognition*, pages 247–265. Springer.

John Rogers Searle. 1969. *Speech acts : an essay in the philosophy of language*. Cambridge University Press.

Gerd Stumme, Rafik Taouil, Yves Bastide, Nicolas Pasquier, and Lotfi Lakhal. 2002. Computing iceberg concept lattices with titanic. *Data & knowledge engineering*, 42(2):189–222.

George Tsatsaronis and Vicky Panagiotopoulou. 2009. A generalized vector space model for text retrieval based on semantic relatedness. In *Proceedings of the 12th Conference of the European Chapter of the Association for Computational Linguistics: Student Research Workshop*, pages 70–78. Association for Computational Linguistics.

Dean van der Merwe, Sergei Obiedkov, and Derrick Kourie. 2004. Addintent: A new incremental algorithm for constructing concept lattices. In Peter Eklund, editor, *Concept Lattices*, volume 2961 of *Lecture Notes in Computer Science*, pages 372–385. Springer Berlin Heidelberg.

SK Michael Wong, Wojciech Ziarko, and Patrick CN Wong. 1985. Generalized vector spaces model in information retrieval. In *Proceedings of the 8th annual international ACM SIGIR conference on Research and development in information retrieval*, pages 18–25. ACM.

Oren Zamir and Oren Etzioni. 1998. Web document clustering: A feasibility demonstration. In *Proceedings of the 21st annual international ACM SIGIR conference on Research and development in information retrieval*, pages 46–54. ACM.

Oren Zamir and Oren Etzioni. 1999. Grouper: a dynamic clustering interface to web search results. *Computer Networks*, 31(11):1361–1374.

Hua-Jun Zeng, Qi-Cai He, Zheng Chen, Wei-Ying Ma, and Jinwen Ma. 2004. Learning to cluster web search results. In *Proceedings of the 27th annual international ACM SIGIR conference on Research and development in information retrieval*, pages 210–217. ACM.

# To Do or Not to Do: the Role of Agendas for Action in Analyzing News Coverage of Violent Conflict

**Katsiaryna Stalpouskaya**
Ludwig-Maximilian University
Oettingen Strasse 67
80337 Munich
katya.stolpovskaya@ifkw.lmu.de

**Christian Baden**
Hebrew University of Jerusalem
Mount Scopus Campus
91905 Jerusalem
c.baden@mail.huji.ac.il

## Abstract

One critical function that news narratives perform is orienting action: Providing a selective, coherent account of events, they suggest what needs to be done, coordinating and motivating public agendas. The importance of news narratives' agendas for action has been particularly salient in the coverage of conflict[1] (Wolfsfeld 1997, Robinson *et al.* 2010): Conflict spurns heated debates wherein advocated courses of action collide, while audiences rely heavily on various media to comprehend ongoing events. Keeping track of the cacophony of agendas advanced in print and online newspapers and magazines, social media, and other public discourse confronts news readers, journalists, decision makers, and scholars alike with a major challenge. Computer assisted analyses have the potential to help comprehending conflict news, distilling agendas for action and possibly predicting the mobilization of consensus and collective action (Snow and Benford 1988). This paper presents the INFOCORE consortium's ongoing efforts at automatically capturing agendas in conflict discourse, employing NLP technology and statistical analysis. We demonstrate the utility and potential of our approach using coverage of the Syrian chemical weapons crisis in 2013.

## 1 Introduction

Frame analysis is long established as one mainstream approach to the analysis of news narratives in communications and links to numerous traditions also in the humanities (Tewksbury and Scheufele 2009, Lakoff 2004, Souders and Dillard 2014). Focusing on the variety of narratives constructed to interpret the same news reality, its power lies in highlighting how different narratives influence audiences' beliefs, attitudes and actions. Specifically, Entman's (1993) seminal definition of frames posits the recommendation of specific treatments as one of four frames' primary functions. However, while numerous scientists (Snow and Benford 1988, Gamson 1995, Giugni 2006, Sanfilippo *et al.* 2008) have underscored frames' motivational and mobilizing functions, there has been remarkably little research on *how* frames advance specific agendas. Despite ample evidence documenting the public agenda setting power of the news (McCombs 2005), its direct antecedent – the agendas for action embedded in the news narrative – have been operationalized crudely as broad topics, or captured laboriously in highly case-bound studies. Computational linguistics have approached the frame analysis of the news texts by identifying the sentiment of articles (cf. Godbole, Srinivasaiah, and Skiena 2007, Scholz and Conrad 2013), and capturing places, people and events as frame elements using named entity recognition technique (Lloyd, Kechagias, and Skiena 2005, Best *et al.* 2006). Frames' mobilizing component, however, has thus far eluded systematic study in humanities, social sciences and computational linguistics. In this paper, we present the

[1] We deploy the definition of a conflict by Gantzel & Schwinghammer (2000): a violent mass conflict is settled by two or more armed forces that perform violence in not a sporadic or spontaneous way.



*Proceedings of the First Workshop on Computing News Storylines*, pages 21–29,
Beijing, China, July 31, 2015. 

INFOCORE[1] consortium's computer-assisted strategy for detecting and classifying agendas for action, which overcomes this limitation.

## 2 INFOCORE's approach to computing news storylines

In the news, conflict is described on several levels of abstraction. On the lowest level, the actors, objectives, aims and other relevant ideas in the given conflict are positioned, and specific *evidential claims* about these are presented, informing readers what is reportedly the case. At the next level, *interpretative frames* contextualize these claims, suggesting how the reported facts are to be interpreted. Combined into complex narratives to meaningfully link sequences of events, these frames finally advance specific *agendas for action* required to bring the conflict narrative to closure (Baden 2014): Integrating the available information to make sense of the situation, frames' motivational function translates the specific understanding of the news narrative into concrete, applicable agendas. Extracting these agendas, in this paper, we thus focus on news storylines' ability to direct action, constituting one primary societal effect of the news.

### 2.2 Agendas for action

From a semantic point of view, agendas for action consist of three components: First, as amply documented by agenda setting research, the issue to be acted upon has to be identified. Second, there needs to be a specific expression of a need to act. Third, the mandated course of action needs to be specified. While the range of relevant issues is principally unbounded and must be determined for each studied context, research in both linguistics and communication has emphasized a finite list of common ways for expressing the need to act:

- Commissive, directive and partially expressive speech acts as defined by Searle (1976), with an enhanced list of speech act verbs (Wierzbicka 1987);
- Imperative sentences: *"Fight them!"*;
- Sentences containing modal verbs obliging someone to do something: "*They must obey*";
- Sentences expressing the speaker's dissatisfaction: "*[Sb.] condemned such a motion*" or "*We will not stand this aggression*";
- General expressions that something cannot stand: "*Something should be done*"
- Rhetorical questions: "*Can we accept such a treatment?*";
- Propositions about desirable, but absent states: "*Peace is the only answer*".

The course of action, again, can include virtually any kind of activities and inactivities. It is therefore useful to classify different kinds of actions more broadly. Owing to the focus on conflict-related news, INFOCORE's analysis aims to distinguish the following agenda types:

- peaceful solution/de-escalation – agendas for peace, a ceasefire, to stop fighting, etc.: "*People need to understand that violence is not an acceptable way to solve disputes.*"
- violent solution/escalation – the opposite of the above category includes calls for military action, violence, escalation, etc.: "*...Fatah and Hamas, which Israel deems a terrorist organizations calling for its destruction*"
- involvement/dialogue/support – including calls for cooperation, negotiations as well as all sorts of help and support: "*Eradication of poverty should be the main priority of humanitarian action.*"
- punishment/sanctions/toughness – the opposite of the previous category, calling for a tough stance and (non-violent) coercion: "*UN official applauds sentencing of militia leader for war crimes.*"
- general/rhetorical questions – agendas that do not call for something specific, but express dissatisfaction with the status quo that should be changed: "*Now is the time to take action.*"
- multiclass – complex treatments wherein multiple clauses express different agenda: "*The international community must break that habit, accept the Palestinian membership application, guarantee Palestinians a war crimes case, prioritize peace and end Israel's impunity - or see international law perverted further in ways that is certain to harm the entire world.*"
- negative – calls for not doing something: "*We must not lower our guard, at any time,*

[1] (In)forming conflict prevention, response, and resolution: The role of media in violent conflict, www.infocore.eu

*Prime Minister Manuel Valls told Parliament, adding that "serious and very high risks remain*". Such agendas may be also expressed without using negators: "*The Department of State warns U.S. citizens of the risks of travel to eastern Ukraine*". Sentences criticizing others for doing something also belong here: "*We condemn these barbaric crimes.*"

- other – sentences that contain an agenda for action but are semantically ambiguous are classified here: "*The militants who massacred schoolchildren, beheaded soldiers and attacked defense installations have surely committed war crimes and must be dealt with as such.*"

As expressing agendas for action necessarily takes propositional form, the task may be formulated as sentence classification. We apply a two-step classification procedure: We identify those sentences expressing an agenda for action in the first step, and classify the expressed agenda by type in a second step. For the present paper, we apply a simplified classification of agenda types: peaceful and dialogic agendas are merged into "cooperative" treatments, while violent and punitive agendas constitute "restrictive" treatments, and the rest fall under "other".

## 3 Related work

Our approach builds upon recent advances in automated content analysis and extraction of frames, as well as in sentence classification. In communication research, automated approaches to frame analysis mostly rely on a detection of co-occurrence patterns: Following Entman's (1993) frame definition, Matthes and Kohring (2008) identify frame elements manually and collate frames based on the systematic joint appearance of these elements (see also Wettstein 2014, Hughes, Lancaster, and Spicer 2011). Kutter and Kantner (2011) rely on an operationalization of semantic fields (Gliozzo and Strapparava 2009) to perform a semi-automated, corpus-based analysis of semantic co-occurrences. Baden (2010) measures frames as "areas of heightened density in a semantic network" (page 90) of systematic, dyadic concept co-occurrences. Sanfilippo *et al.* (2008) depart from an extended frame definition and extract frame components (Promoter, Intention, Target, Issue, etc.) using different NLP techniques (grammar parsing, NER, co-reference and temporal resolution). In order to measure Intention, they also capture *intent* verbs, which are directly related to our approach in the current paper.

Relevant work on sentence classification has focused on assessing different classification algorithms and fine-tuning their parameters and features (Kim 2014, Khoo, Marom, and Albrecht 2006, Revathi *et al.* 2012), for application to specific tasks and domains (Cohen, Carvalho, and Mitchell 2004, Qadir and Riloff 2011, Kim, Martinez, and Cavedon 2011, McKnight and Srinivasan 2003). Most applicable here are those studies classifying text segments as speech acts: Cohen, Carvalho, and Mitchell (2004) categorize whole email messages as requests, proposals, amends, commitments, deliveries, and other speech acts. Using TFIDF-weighted bag of words, bigrams, and POS-tags, they compare four classifiers – Voted Perceptron, AdaBoost, SVM, Decision Tree – the latter two outperforming the rest.

Qadir and Riloff (2011) finally move the categorization task to sentence level, assigning speech act labels as defined by Searle (1976) to message board posts. Their approach also reflects grammatical structure of sentences in features (e.g., capturing imperative sentences and disambiguating them from interrogative ones), which were used to train a SVM classifier. While we are not interested here in representatives or expressives that do not advance specific agendas, their classification strategy is closely related to ours; however, we also included instances that merely imply an agenda for action, but fall short of forming classic directives. To our knowledge, ours presents the first study to comprehensively distil agendas, including also speech-act-like structures, in conflict news coverage to date.

## 4 Methodology

### 4.1 Corpus

To train the classifier, we manually annotated a 1723-sentence corpus, labeling each sentence as "cooperative treatment" (287 items), "restrictive treatment" (204 items), "other" (249 items) or "none" (983 items). For the first round of classification the former three categories are combined. For the second round, the "none" category was excluded from the pool of sentences. The LexisNexis[1] database was used for crafting the corpus, retrieving all English language sources including the keywords "conflict", "war" or "violence" from 1 January to 1 March 2015. Articles were split into sentences and labeled accordingly.

### 4.2 Features

For both rounds of classification, n-gram features with n between 1 and 3 were used. For the second round the words were stemmed, as it improved the performance in the second round but not in the first: To classify a sentence as containing an agenda, not only lexical, but also grammatical information is important, which is contained in endings and suffixes. Also stop-words removal – a classical pre-processing step in NLP – was not performed as it reduces performance: stop-word lists usually include prepositions, particles, articles and auxiliary words which contain important grammatical information needed for such classification (Khoo, Marom, and Albrecht 2006). By contrast, recognizing the agenda type is a purely semantic classification task, for which stems are sufficient. Features extraction and model training was carried out using the Weka toolkit for data mining (Hall *et al.* 2009).

### 4.3 Classifiers

We compared the results of three classification algorithms – decision tree (J48), Naïve Bayes Multinomial (NBM) and support vector machine (SVM) - to find out which one performs best. Cross validation with 5 and 3 folds was used for the first and the second rounds respectively. For the first round, SVM outperformed the rest, classifying 74% of instances correctly (see Table 1).

| | Precision | Recall | F1 |
|---|---|---|---|
| J48 | 0.70 | 0.70 | 0.70 |
| NBM | 0.73 | 0.72 | 0.73 |
| SVM | 0.74 | 0.74 | 0.72 |

*Table 1: Weighted average Precision, Recall and F-measure scores for decision tree, Naïve Bayes Multinomial and support vector machine for the classification of agendas vs. non-agendas.*

For the second round, SVM and NBM performed equally well: 52% of instances were classified correctly (see Table 2). Poor classification results may be explained by little amount of training data and high semantic ambiguity of the concept.

| | Precision | Recall | F1 |
|---|---|---|---|
| J48 | 0.48 | 0.48 | 0.48 |
| NBM | 0.52 | 0.52 | 0.52 |
| SVM | 0.52 | 0.52 | 0.52 |

*Table 2: Weighted average Precision, Recall and F-measure scores for decision tree, Naïve Bayes Multinomial and support vector machine for the classification of agendas as cooperative, restrictive and other.*

Generally, our results support the findings of Khoo, Marom and Albrecht (2006) that SVM is the most powerful algorithm for sentence level classification.

## 5 Computing the storyline of news coverage of Syrian chemical weapons crises

### 5.1 The Story

Extracting agendas for action from the news coverage on violent conflict helps tracking the dynamics of a conflict, identifying and possibly predicting phases of escalation and de-escalation: Dominantly expressed agendas not only prepare news audiences for impending policy moves and collective action in conflict, they also reflect preeminent interpretations of current conflict as accessible to or beyond peaceful resolution. Conflict events extend ongoing news narratives, update conflict perceptions, and shift conflict policy agendas. The Syrian chemical weapons (CW) crisis 2013 progressed from initial rumors, uncertainty and global hesitation in March, through rapid escalation following the large scale CW attacks in Ghouta in August, culminating in projected

[1] www.nexis.com

imminent US air strikes, to international disengagement following Syria's surrender of its CW arsenals to UN control in October, and their destruction by the OPCW. Widely diverse agendas were discussed at all times, but only few became dominant temporarily (for more in depth analysis of news coverage of the crises see Baden and Stalpouskaya 2015).

### 5.2 Material

For our analysis, we used news coverage of the Syrian CW crisis in the British Guardian and the American New York Times (NYT). Both media act as papers of record for the respective countries, key global players in the crisis, closely observing their foreign policy debates. The coverage was retrieved from the respective news archives based on a search for references to Syria (e.g. "Syria", "Damascus") and chemical weapons (e.g. "chemical weapon", "sarin", "WMD"). The dataset comprised 584 articles from the Guardian and 609 from NYT. Articles were grouped by month, split into sentences, and each sentence classified based on the two-step procedure and pre-trained SVM classifier described above.

### 5.3 Results

The analysis reveals a steady presence of agendas, which are detected in one third of all sentences throughout the entire time range (Table 3). Figure 1 shows that there are initially fewer agendas expressed in the UK, whose role in the conflict crystallizes only once premier Cameron calls for active intervention, building steadily as the debate picks up speed; however, when the UK's parliament votes against intervention, the need to discuss an active British role ceases, the administrative attention wanders on, and the share of agendas expressed in the Guardian wanes. By contrast, the NYT considers Syria a case for possible US intervention from the outset (reflecting Obama's "red line"[1]), and discusses policy options long before the administration openly considers military action. The role of agendas in the coverage is high at all times. Interestingly, the share remains stable despite major changes in the amount of attention to the crisis, culminating in September as the Ghouta attacks initiate a hectic search for viable action (less so in the UK, where military action is now off the table).

Looking at the kinds of agendas distinguished in Figure 2, political, cooperative efforts dominate at all times over military options (the spike of restrictive agendas in the Guardian's coverage in July overrepresents few calls for arming rebels and cited militants during a month of very low coverage). In the US, support for military action builds slowly but steadily, while the White House's justification of its hesitant stance results in many calls for forging international agreement and alliances on Syria. Culminating in July, the US adopt a more unilateral stance after Ghouta, when cooperative agendas drop and calls for independent investigation (other) dominate. Following the US' adoption of Russia's plan to put Syria's CW under UN control, also restrictive agendas drop, while monitoring compliance becomes the primary concern. In the Guardian, many calls for military action exist at the outset, but are quickly diffused into a more general punitive agenda ("stopping Assad", "not standing by idly", classified as "other") as rumors solidify. While the UK waits for the US to take the lead, agreement that someone urgently needs to find some solution builds, but Cameron's military agenda remains at a share of one fifth as only one of many such proposals. In both papers, the resolve to escalate the crisis is perceptibly limited: Even after the Ghouta attacks, when patience with global diplomacy finally fails and the US are at the verge of ordering missile strikes, cooperative agendas remain more salient than restrictive ones. And while the tone is notably more hostile toward Assad in the Guardian, the vagueness of agendas correctly indicates that no specific action is imminent.

---

[1] The New York Times 16.01.2013. *Consulate Supported Claim of Syria Gas Attack, Report Says.* http://www.nytimes.com/2013/01/16/world/middleeast/consulate-said-to-support-claim-of-syrian-gas-attack.html

| | | Jan | Feb | Mar | Apr | May | Jun | Jul | Aug | Sep | Oct |
|---|---|---|---|---|---|---|---|---|---|---|---|
| The Guardian | Total sentences | 308 | 243 | 674 | 595 | 1259 | 1342 | 44 | 4158 | 7079 | 1174 |
| | Agendas | 62 | 30 | 161 | 174 | 344 | 405 | 16 | 1220 | 1889 | 269 |
| | Agendas (%) | 20.1 | 12.3 | 23.9 | 29.2 | 27.3 | 30.2 | 36.4 | 29.3 | 26.7 | 22.9 |
| | cooperative | 22 | 11 | 53 | 55 | 127 | 137 | 2 | 430 | 675 | 104 |
| | cooperative (%) | 35.5 | 36.7 | 32.9 | 31.6 | 36.9 | 33.8 | 12.5 | 35.2 | 35.7 | 38.7 |
| | restrictive | 14 | 8 | 37 | 25 | 51 | 67 | 6 | 248 | 355 | 50 |
| | restrictive (%) | 22.6 | 26.7 | 23.0 | 14.4 | 14.8 | 16.5 | 37.5 | 20.3 | 18.8 | 18.6 |
| | other | 26 | 11 | 71 | 94 | 165 | 200 | 8 | 542 | 859 | 115 |
| | other (%) | 41.9 | 36.7 | 44.1 | 54.0 | 48.0 | 49.4 | 50.0 | 44.4 | 45.5 | 42.8 |
| New York Times | Total sentences | 832 | 585 | 1092 | 1772 | 2432 | 1252 | 355 | 3126 | 12894 | 2690 |
| | Agendas | 199 | 188 | 322 | 433 | 760 | 428 | 119 | 1013 | 4178 | 728 |
| | Agendas (%) | 23.9 | 32.1 | 29.5 | 24.4 | 31.3 | 34.2 | 33.5 | 32.4 | 32.4 | 27.1 |
| | cooperative | 73 | 77 | 99 | 157 | 292 | 172 | 55 | 332 | 1607 | 281 |
| | cooperative (%) | 36.7 | 41.0 | 30.7 | 36.3 | 38.4 | 40.2 | 46.2 | 32.8 | 38.5 | 38.6 |
| | restrictive | 36 | 30 | 67 | 99 | 146 | 104 | 30 | 260 | 784 | 144 |
| | restrictive (%) | 18.1 | 16.0 | 20.8 | 22.9 | 19.2 | 24.3 | 25.2 | 25.7 | 18.8 | 19.8 |
| | other | 90 | 81 | 156 | 177 | 322 | 152 | 34 | 421 | 1787 | 303 |
| | other (%) | 45.2 | 43.1 | 48.4 | 40.9 | 42.4 | 35.5 | 28.6 | 41.6 | 42.8 | 41.6 |

*Table 3: Classification Results for Agendas for Action and Agenda Types in Guardian and NYT*

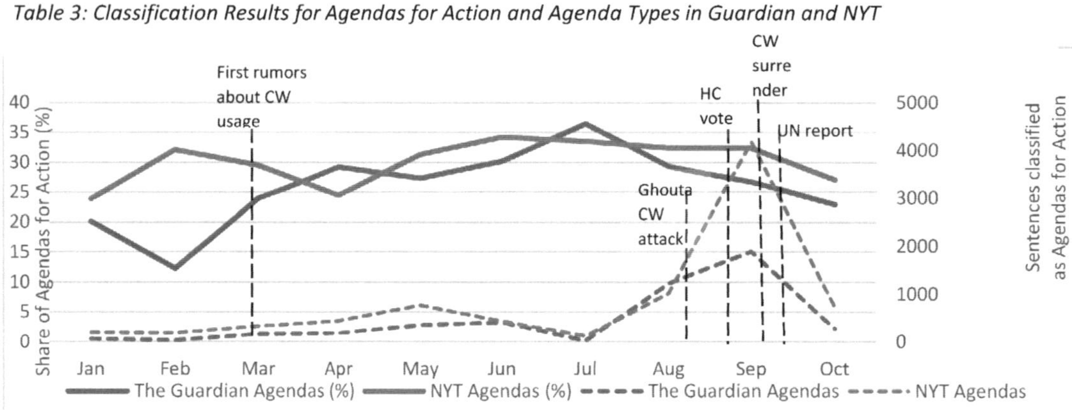


*Figure 1: Total Amount and Share of Sentences Classified as Agendas for Action in Guardian and NYT*

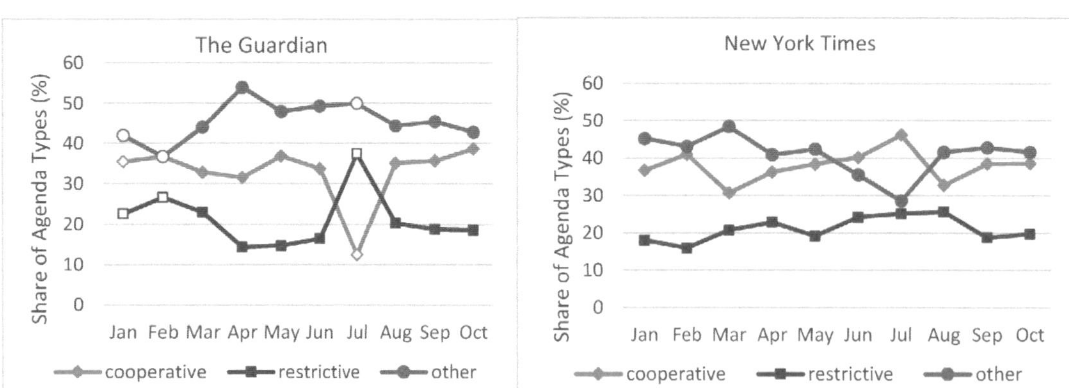


*Figure 2: Distribution of Agenda Types for cooperative, restrictive, and other treatment*

Note: Classifications based on fewer than 100 sentences with hollow markers

## 6 Limitations and future work

The present study remains work in progress in important ways. First, the data presented uses a simplified classification of agendas and does not yet integrate with the analysis of frames and evidential claims underway within the INFOCORE project. Second, we do not yet capture certain implicit agendas for action, whose illocutionary force indirectly constitutes a perlocutionary act (Austin 1962) e.g., "we see these violations with grave concern". Such agendas rely on conventional values to unfold their directive qualities, and therefore require different operational strategies. Third, we only detect agendas for action contained within one sentence, yet, one sentence may contain several agendas, and agendas span multiple sentences. The former case is classified as "multiclass" in our fine classification, but allows further differentiation. To detect agendas spanning sentences, tools are needed that tie together sentences based on anaphora resolution, conjunctions such as "also", "as well", or identity chains of synonymous predicates.

Furthermore, with the current set-up, fine classification performs poorly: the best accuracy achieved was 36% using NBM. More training data is needed, but also utilizing lexical resources (e.g., WordNet) should boost precision and recall. Similarly, grammatical ambiguity is responsible for some misclassification of agendas vs. non-agendas (e.g., "they request" vs. "request is being processed") and requires resolution using additional NLP resources.

Finally, to get the full picture of the news storyline, agendas for action need to be linked to the speaker advancing and others commenting upon that agenda. While strategies exist for most of the named limitations, bringing them to bear on our analysis remains a task for future work.

## 7 Conclusion

Our goal was to highlight the role of "agendas for action" as one key, socially relevant conclusion arising from competing news storylines, and propose a strategy for detecting these algorithmically in a text corpus. Related, but not identical to directive speech acts, the approach pursued by the INFOCORE consortium combines grammatical and semantic resources to classify relevant statements in the news. Our focus on agendas bridges a gap in the study of news content and discourse, which often postulates the action coordinating and directing role of new narratives, but has focused much more on the descriptive semantic qualities of news frames than on their mobilizing capacities. Agendas for action present the critical link between discursive representations and social action, but have to date mostly evaded scholarly attention. Identifying common ways of suggesting specific courses of action, we applied machine learning technique to extract sentences expressing agendas for action. Currently standard n-rams with n between 1 and 3 were used as features. In a number of trials, we found large margin classifiers to perform best, and applied the trained model to analyze news coverage of Syrian CW crisis in 2013. Sentences were classified in two steps, first discriminating agendas for action from statements without directive force, and qualifying the nature of the advocated treatment in the second step. The procedure demonstrates the potential of combining grammatical and semantic information for sentence classification, and opens up avenues for further research. We found consistently high percentages of agendas expressed in the news, advocating different kinds of action at different moments during the crisis. The extracted agendas are informative about the quality of news debates about the conflict, and can be tied to actual policies and developments within the crisis. However, further work is needed to increase differentiation, accuracy, and critically, to integrate the detected agendas into the context of the news storyline.

## References


Austin, John L. 1962. *How to do things with words: The William James Lectures delivered at Harvard University in 1955.* Harvard University Press, Cambridge.

Baden, Christian. 2014. Constructions of violent conflict in public discourse: Conceptual framework for the content & discourse analytic perspective (within WP5, WP6, WP7, & WP8). INFOCORE Working Paper: www.infocore.eu/results/

Baden, Christian. 2010. Communication, contextualization, & cognition: Patterns &

processes of frames' influence on people's interpretations of the EU Constitution. PhD thesis. VU University, Amsterdam.

Baden, Christian and Stalpouskaya, Katsiaryna. 2015. Maintaining frame coherence between uncertain information and changing agendas: The evolving framing of the Syrian chemical attacks in the US, British, and Russian news. Paper presented at ICA Annual Conference, San Juan.

Best, Clive, Pouliquen, Bruno, Steinberger, Ralf, Van der Goot, Erik, Blackler, Ken, Fuart, Flavio, Oellinger, Tamara, and Ignat, Camelia. 2006. *Towards Automatic Event Tracking. Intelligence and Security Informatics: Lecture Notes in Computer Science*, 3975: 26-34.

Cohen, William. W, Carvalho, Vitor. R., and Mitchell, Tom. M. 2004. Learning to Classify Email into "Speech Acts". In *Proceedings of the 2004 Conference on Empirical Methods in Natural Language Processing*, pages 309-316, Barcelona.

Entman, Robert M. 1993. Framing: Toward clarification of a fractured paradigm. *Journal of Communication*, 43(4): 51-58.

Gamson, William A. 1995. Constructing Social Protest. In H. Johnston and B. Klandermans, editors, *Social Movements and Culture,* University of Minnesota Press, Minneapolis, pages 85–106.

Gantzel, Klaus J. and Schwinghammer, Torsten. 2000. *Warfare since the Second World War*. Transaction, New Brunswick.

Giugni, Marco. 2006. Problem Framing and Collective Action in the field of Unemployment. Paper presented at International conference on Contentious Politics and Social Movements in the 21th century.

Gliozzo, Alfio and Strapparava, Carlo. 2009. *Semantic domains in computational linguistics*. Springer, Berlin.

Godbole, Namrata, Srinivasaiah, Manjunath, and Skiena, Steven. 2007. Large-scale sentiment analysis for news and blogs. Paper presented at the International Conference on Weblogs and Social Media, Colorado.

Hall, Mark, Frank, Eibe, Holmes, Geoffrey, Pfahringer, Bernhard, Reutemann, Peter, and Witten, Ian H. 2009. The weka data mining software: an update. *SIGKDD Explor. Newsl.* 11:10–18.

Hughes, Caitlin E., Lancaster, Kari, and Spicer, Bridget. 2011. How do Australian news media depict illicit drug issues?: An analysis of print media reporting across and between illicit drugs, 2003-2008. *International Journal of Drug Policy*, 22(4): 285–291.

Khoo, Anthony, Marom, Yuval, and Albrecht, David. 2006. Experiments with Sentence Classification. In *Proceedings of the 2006 Australasian language technology workshop*, pages 18-25, Sydney.

Kim, Su N., Martinez, David, and Cavedon, Lawrence. 2011. Automatic Classification of Sentences to Support Evidence Based Medicine. In *DTMBIO '10 Proceedings of the ACM Fourth International Workshop on Data and Text Mining in Biomedical Informatics*, pages 13-22, New York.

Kim, Yoon. 2014. Convolutional Neural Networks for Sentence Classification. In *Proceedings of the 2014 Conference on Empirical Methods in Natural Language Processing*, pages 1746-1752, Doha.

Kutter, Amelie and Kantner, Cathleen. 2011. Corpus-based content analysis: A method for investigating news coverage on war and intervention. Retrieved from http://www.uni-stuttgart.de/soz/ib/forschung/IRWorkingPapers/IROWP_Series_2012_1_Kutter_Kantner_Corpus-Based_Content_Analysis.pdf

Lakoff, George. 2004. *Don't think of an elephant!: Know your values and frame the debate: The essential guide for progressives.* Chelsea Green Publishing, White River.

Lloyd, Levon, Kechagias, Dimitrios, and Skiena, Steven. 2005. Lydia: A system for large-scale news analysis. *String Processing and Information Retrieval: Volume Lecture Notes in Computer Science*, 3772:161-166.

Matthes, Jörg and Kohring, Matthias. 2008. The Content Analysis of Media Frames: Toward Improving Reliability and Validity. *Journal of Communication*, 58(2): 258–279.

McCombs, Maxwell E. 2005. A Look at Agenda-setting: past, present and future. *Journalism Studies*, 6(4): 543-557.

McCombs and Shaw. 1993. The evolution of Agenda-Setting Research: Twenty-Five Years in the Marketplace of Ideas. *Journal of Communication*, 43(2): 58-67.

McKnight, Larry and Srinivasan, Padmini. 2003. Categorization of Sentence Types in Medical Abstracts. In Proceedings of AMIA Annual Symposium, pages 440-444, Washington.

Qadir, Ashequl and Riloff, Ellen. (2011). Classifying Sentences as Speech Acts in Message Board Posts. In *Proceedings of the 2011 Conference on Empirical Methods in Natural Language Processing,* pages 748-759, Edinburgh.

Revathi, T., Ramya, L.V., Tanuja, M., Pavani, S., and Swathi, M. 2012. Sentence Level Semantic Classification of Online Product Reviews of Mixed Opinions Using Naïve bayes Classifier.

*International Journal of Engineering Trends and Technology*, 3(2): 127-132.

Robinson, Piers, Goddard, Peter, Parry, Katy, and Murray, Craig. 2010. *Pockets of resistance: British news media, war and theory in the 2003 invasion of Iraq*. Manchester University Press, Manchester.

Sanfilippo, Antonio, Franklin, Lyndsey, Tratz, Stephen, Danielson, Gary, Mileson, Nicholas, Riensche, Roderick, and McGrath, Liam. 2008. Automating Frame Analysis. In H. Liu, J. J. Salerno, M. J. Young, editors, *Social Computing, Behavioral Modeling, and Prediction*. Springer, Tempe, pages 239-249.

Scholz, Thomas and Conrad, Stefan. 2013. Opinion Mining in Newspaper Articles by Entropy-based Word Connections. In *Proceedings of the 2013 Conference on Empirical Methods in Natural Language Processing*, pages 1828–1839, Seattle.

Searle, John R. 1976. A classification of illocutionary acts. *Language in Society*, 5(1): 1–23.

Snow, David A. and Benford, Robert D. 1988. Ideology, Frame Resonance, and Participant Mobilization. *International Social Movement Research*, 1(1): 197–217.

Souders, Michael. C. and Dillard, Kara N. 2014. Framing Connections: An Essay on Improving the Relationship between Rhetorical and Social Scientific Frame Studies, Including a Study of G. W. Bush's Framing of Immigration. *International Journal of Communication*, 8: 1008-1028.

Tewksbury, David and Scheufele, Dietram A. 2009. News framing theory and research. In J. Bryant and M. B. Oliver, editors, *Media effects: Advances in theory and research.* Routledge, New York, pages 17-33.

Wettstein, Martin. 2014. Content analysis of mediated public debates: Methodological framework for a computer-assisted quantitative content analysis. National Centre of Competence in Research: Challenges to Democracy in the 21st Century, Working Paper 74.

Wierzbicka, Anna. 1987. *English speech act verbs: a semantic dictionary*. Academic Press, Sydney.

Wolfsfeld, Gadi. 1997. *Media and political conflict: News from the Middle East.* Cambridge University Press, Cambridge.

# MediaMeter: A Global Monitor for Online News Coverage

**Tadashi Nomoto**
National Institute of Japanese Literature
10-3 Modori Tachikawa, Japan
nomoto@acm.org

## Abstract

This paper introduces MediaMeter, an application that works to detect and track emergent topics in the US online news media. What makes MediaMeter unique is its reliance on a labeling algorithm which we call WikiLabel, whose primary goal is to identify what news stories are about by looking up Wikipedia. We discuss some of the major news events that were successfully detected and how it compares to prior work.

## 1 Introduction

A long term goal of this project is to build a socio-logically credible computational platform that enables the user to observe how social agenda evolve and spread across the globe and across the media, as they happen. To this end, we have built a prototype system we call MediaMeter, which is designed to detect and track trending topics in the online US news media. One important feature of the system lies in its making use of and building upon a particular approach called WikiLabel (Nomoto, 2011). The idea was to identify topics of a document by mapping it into a conceptual space derived from Wikipedia, which consists of finding a Wikipedia page similar to the document and taking its page title as a possible topic label. Further, to deal with events not known to Wikipedia, it is equipped with the capability of re-creating a page title so as to make it better fit the content of the document. In the following, we look at what WikiLabel does and how it works before we discuss MediaMeter.

## 2 WikiLabel

WikiLabel takes as input a document which one likes to have labeled, and outputs a ranked list of label candidates along with the confidence scores.

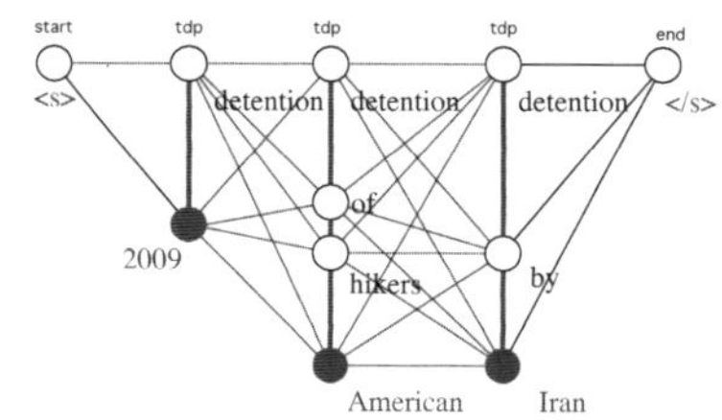


Figure 1: Trellis for enumerating compressions for *"2009 detention of American hikers by Iran"*.

The document it takes as input needs to be in the form of a vector space model (VSM). Now assume that $\vec{\theta}$ represents a VSM of document $d$. Let us define $l^*_{\vec{\theta}}$, a likely topic label for $d$, as follows.

$$l^*_{\vec{\theta}} = \underset{l:p[l] \in \mathcal{U}}{\arg\max}\, \mathrm{Prox}(p[l], \vec{\theta}|_N), \tag{1}$$

where $p[l]$ denotes a Wikipedia page with a title $l$ and $\vec{\theta}|_N$ a VSM with its elements limited to top $N$ terms in $d$ (as measured by TFIDF). $\mathrm{Prox}(p[l], \vec{\theta}|_N)$ is given by:

$$\mathrm{Prox}(p[l], \vec{\theta}|_N) = \lambda Sr(p[l], \vec{\theta}|_N) + (1-\lambda) Lo(l, \vec{\theta}).$$

We let:

$$Sr(\mathbf{r}, \mathbf{q}) = \left(1 + \sum_t^N (\mathbf{q}(t) - \mathbf{r}(t))^2\right)^{-1}$$

and

$$Lo(l, \vec{v}) = \frac{\sum_i^{|l|} I(l[i], \mathbf{v})}{|\, l \,|} - 1$$

where $I(w, v) = 1$ if $w \in v$ and 0 otherwise.

$Sr(\vec{x}, \vec{y})$ represents the distance between $\vec{x}$ and $\vec{y}$, normalized to vary between 0 and 1. $Lo(l, \vec{v})$ measures how many terms $l$ and $\vec{v}$ have in common, intended to quantify the relevance of $l$ to $\vec{v}$. $l[i]$ indicates $i$-th term in $l$. Note that $Lo$ works as a penalizing term: if one finds all the terms $l$ has in $\vec{v}$, there will be no penalty: if not, there will



*Proceedings of the First Workshop on Computing News Storylines*, pages 30–34,
Beijing, China, July 31, 2015. 

Table 1: Compressing a Wikipedia title

| 2009 detention of American hikers by Iran |
|---|
| 2009 detention |
| 2009 detention by Iran |
| 2009 detention of hikers |
| 2009 detention of hikers by Iran |
| 2009 detention of American hikers by Iran |
| ... |

Table 2: Summary of the quality review by humans. '#instances' refers to the number of labels sent to judges for evaluation.

| LANGUAGE | RATING | #instances |
|---|---|---|
| ENGLISH | 4.63 | 97 |
| JAPANESE | 4.41 | 92 |

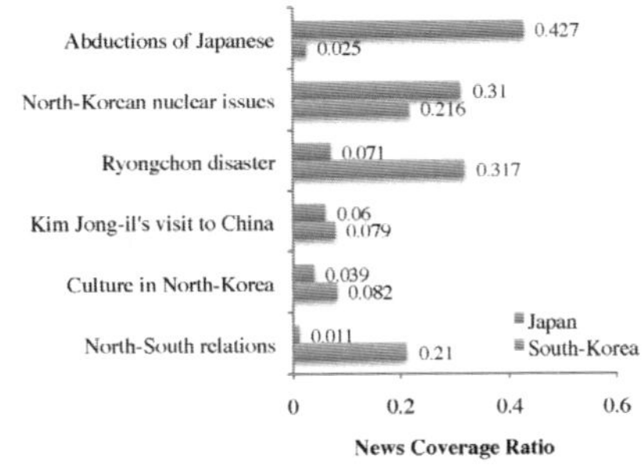


Figure 2: Conflicting media perceptions of North-Korea (E Gwangho, 2006). 'News coverage ratio' indicates the proportion of news articles focusing on a particular topic.

be a penalty, the degree of which depends on the number of terms in $l$ that are missing in $\vec{v}$. $\mathcal{U}$ represents the entire set of pages in Wikipedia whose namespace is 0. We refer to an approach based on the model in Eqn. 1 as 'WikiLabel.' We note that the prior work by Nomoto (2011) which the current approach builds on, is equivalent to the model in Eqn. 1 with $\lambda$ set to 1.

One important feature of the present version, which is not shared by the previous one, is its ability to go beyond Wikipedia page titles: if it comes across a news story with a topic unknown to Wikipedia, WikiLabel will generalize a relevant page title by removing parts of it that are not warranted by the story, while making sure that its grammar stays intact. A principal driver of this process is sentence compression, which works to shorten a sentence or phrase, using a trellis created from a corresponding dependency structure (e.g. Figure 1). Upon receiving possible candidates from sentence compression, WikiLabel turns to the formula in Eqn. 1 and in particular, $Lo$[1] to determine a compression that best fits the document in question.

## 3 North-Korean Agenda

Shown in Figure 3 are most popular topics WikiLabel found among news stories discussing North Korea (DPRK), published online in 2011, in a number of different countries, including US, South-Korea and Japan (the number of stories we covered was 2,230 (US), 2,271 (South-Korea), and 2,815 (Japan)). Labels in the panels are given as they are generated by WikiLabel, except those for the Japanese media, which are translated from Japanese. (The horizontal axis in each panel represents the proportion of stories on a given topic.) Notice that there are interesting discrepancies among the countries in the way they talk about North Korea: the US tends to see DPRK as a nuclear menace while South Korea focuses on diplomatic and humanitarian issues surrounding North Korea; the Japanese media, on the other hand, depict the country as if it had nothing worth talking about except nuclear issues and its abduction of the Japanese. Table 2 shows how two human assessors, university graduates, rated on average, the quality of labels generated by WikiLabel for articles discussing North-Korea, on a scale of 1 (poor) to 5 (good), for English and Japanese.

Curiously, a study on news broadcasts in South Korean and Japan (Gwangho, 2006) found that the South Korean media paid more attention to foreign relations and open-door policies of North Korea, while the Japanese media were mostly engrossed with North Korean abductions of Japanese and nuclear issues. In Figure 2, which reproduces some of his findings, we recognize a familiar tendency of the Japanese media to play up nuclear issues and dismiss North Korea's external relations, which resonate with things we have found here with WikiLabel.

[1] Because the candidates here are all linked to the same Wikipedia page, $Sr$ can be safely ignored as it remains invariant across them.

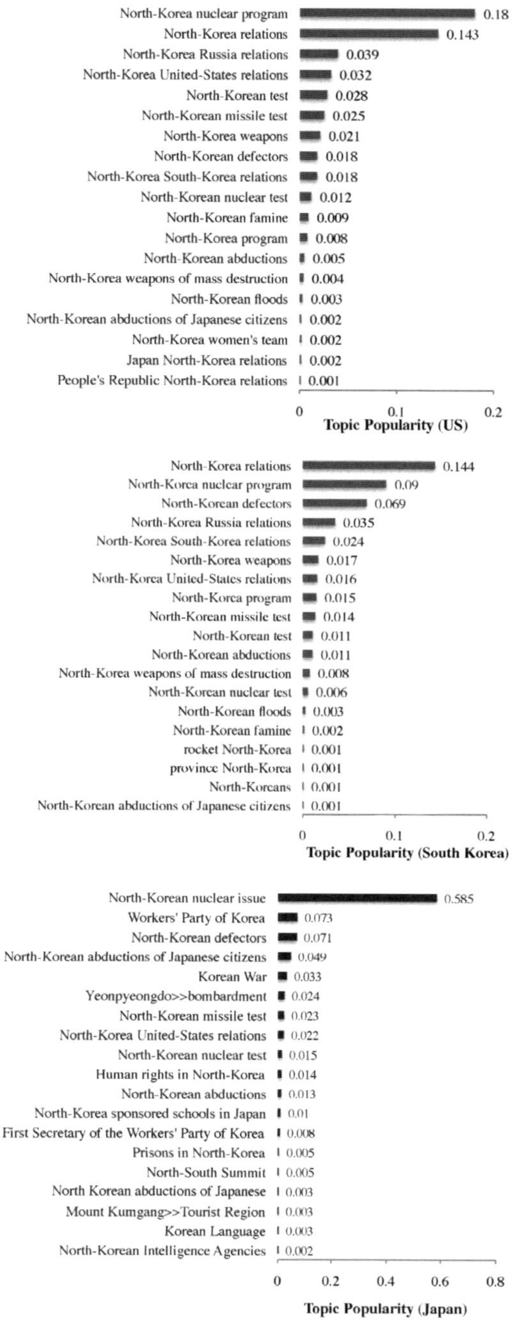


Figure 3: North-Korean agenda across countries

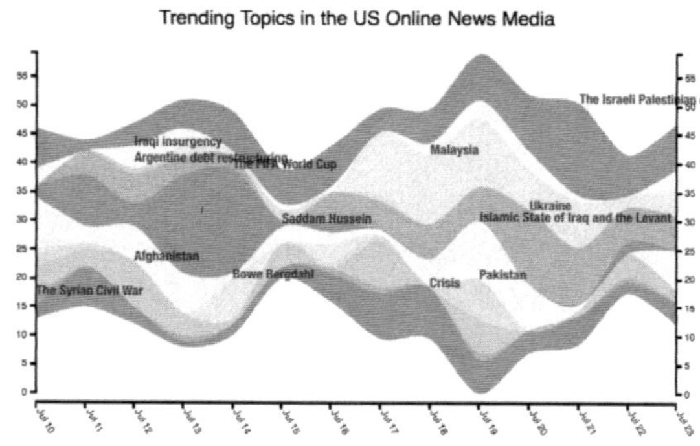


Figure 4: MediaMeter: Overview

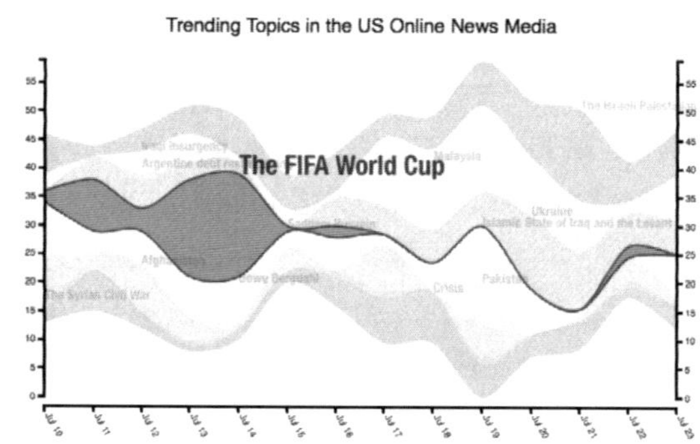


Figure 5: MediaMeter: Focused View 1

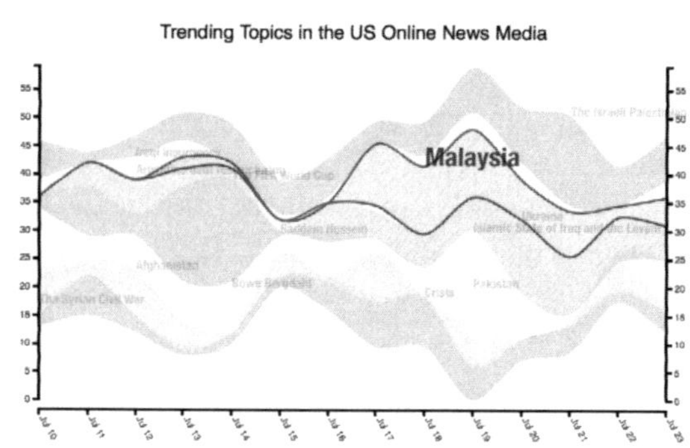


Figure 6: MediaMeter: Focused View 2

## 4 MediaMeter

MediaMeter[2] is a web application that draws on WikiLabel to detect trending topics in the US online news media (which includes CNN, ABC, MSNBC, BBC, Fox, Reuters, Yahoo! News, etc). It is equipped with a visualization capability based on ThemeRiver (Havre et al., 2002; Byron and Wattenberg, 2008), enabling a simultaneous tracking of multiple topics over time. It performs the following routines on a daily basis: (1) collect news stories that appeared during the day; (2) generate topic labels for 600 of them chosen at random; (3) select labels whose score is 1 or above on the burstiness scale (Kleinberg, 2002); (4) find for each of the top ranking labels how many stories carry that label; and (5) plot the numbers using the ThemeRiver, together with the associated labels. Topic labels are placed automatically through integer linear programming (Christensen et al., 1995).

Figure 4 gives a ThemeRiver visualization of trending topics for the period from July 10 to 23, 2014. Figures 5 and 6 show views focusing on particular topics, with the former looking at the World Cup and the latter at Malaysia. The media's attention to the World Cup mushroomed on July 14th, the day when the final match took place, and fizzled out on the following day. Meanwhile, in Figure 6, there is a sudden burst of stories related to Malaysia on July 17th, which coincides with the day when a Malaysian jetliner was shot down over the Ukrainian air space. While it is hard to tell how accurately MediaMeter reflects the reality, our feeling is that it is doing reasonably well in picking up major trends in the US news media.

## 5 Evaluation

To find where we stand in comparison to prior work, we have done some experiments, using TDT-PILOT, NYT2013, and Fox News corpora. TDT-PILOT refers to a corpus containing 15,863 news stories from CNN and Reuters, published between July 1, 1994 and June 30, 1995. The Fox News corpus has the total of 11,014 articles, coming from the online Fox news site, which were published between January, 2015 and April, 2015. NYT2013 consists of articles we collected from the New York Times online between June and December, 2013, totaling 19,952. We measured performance in terms of how well machine generated labels match those by humans, based on the metric known as ROUGE-W (Lin, 2004).[3] ROUGE-W gives a score indicating the degree of similarity between two strings in terms of the length of a subsequence shared by both strings. The score ranges from 0 to 1, with 0 indicating no match and 1 a perfect match. In the experiment, we ran TextRank (TRANK) (Mihalcea and Tarau, 2004) – the current state of the art in topic extraction – and different renditions of WikiLabel: RM1 refers to a model in Eqn 1 with $\lambda$ set to 0.5 and sentence compression turned off; RM1/X is like RM1 except that it makes use of sentence compression; RM0 is a RM1 with $\lambda$ set to 1, disengaging *Lo* altogether.

Table 3: Per-document performance@1

| | TRANK | $RM_0$ | $RM_1$ | $RM_1$/X |
|---|---|---|---|---|
| NYT | 0.000 | 0.056 | 0.056 | **0.069** |
| TDT | 0.030 | 0.042 | 0.048 | **0.051** |
| FOX* | 0.231 | 0.264 | 0.264 | **0.298** |

Table 3 gives a summary of what we found. Numbers in the table denote ROUGE-W scores of relevant systems, averaged over the entire articles in each dataset. Per-document performance@1 means that we consider labels that ranked the first when measuring performance. One note about FOX. FOX has each story labeled with multiple topic descriptors, in contrast to NYT and TDT where we have only one topic label associated with each article. Since there was no intrinsically correct way of choosing among descriptors that FOX provides, we paired up a label candidate with each descriptor and ran ROUGE-W on each of the pairs, taking the highest score we got as a representative of the overall performance. Results in Table 3 clearly corroborate the superiority of RM0 through RM1/X over TextRank.

## 6 Conclusions

In this paper, we looked at a particular approach we call WikiLabel to detecting topics in online news articles, explaining some technical details of how it works, and presented MediaMeter, which showcases WikiLabel in action. We also demonstrated the empirical effectiveness of the approach through experiments with NYT2013, FOX News and TDT-PILOT.

[2] http://www.quantmedia.org/meter/demo.html

[3] Each article in all the three datasets comes with human supplied topic labels.

## References


Lee Byron and Martin Wattenberg. 2008. Stacked graphs - Geometry & Aesthetics. *IEEE Transactions on Visualization and Computer Graphics*, 14(6):1245–1252.

Jon Christensen, Joe Marks, and Stuart Shieber. 1995. An empirical study of algorithms for point-feature label placement. *ACM Trans. Graph.*, 14(3):203–232, July.

E. Gwangho. 2006. *Hutatsu no Kita-Chosen* (Two North Koreas). *Media Communication*, 56:59–71. Keio University.

S. Havre, E. Hetzler, P. Whitney, and L. Nowell. 2002. Themeriver: visualizing thematic changes in large document collections. *Visualization and Computer Graphics, IEEE Transactions on*, 8(1):9–20, Jan.

Jon Kleinberg. 2002. Bursty and hierarchical structure in streams. In *Proceedings of the Eighth ACM SIGKDD International Conference on Knowledge Discovery and Data Mining*, KDD '02, pages 91–101, New York, NY, USA. ACM.

Chin-Yew Lin. 2004. Rouge: a package for automatic evaluation of summaries. In *Proceedings of the Workshop on Text Summarization Branches Out (WAS 2004)*.

Rada Mihalcea and Paul Tarau. 2004. Textrank: Bringing order into texts. Association for Computational Linguistics.

Tadashi Nomoto. 2011. Wikilabel: an encyclopedic approach to labeling documents en masse. In *Proceedings of the 20th ACM international conference on Information and knowledge management*, CIKM '11, pages 2341–2344, New York, NY, USA. ACM.

# Expanding the horizons: adding a new language to the news personalization system

**Andrew Fedorovsky**
News360 Ltd.
afedorovsky@news360.com
**Varvara Litvinova**
News360 Ltd.
vlitvinova@news360.ru
**Darya Trofimova**
News360 Ltd.
dtrofimova@news360.ru
**Maxim Ionov**
News360 Ltd.
max.ionov@gmail.com
**Tatyana Olenina**
News360 Ltd.
tolenina@news360.ru

**Abstract**

News360 is the news aggregation system with personalization. Initially created for English, it was recently adapted for German. In this paper, we show that it is possible to adapt such systems automatically, without any manual labour, using only open knowledge bases and Wikipedia dumps. We propose a method for adaptation named entity linking and classification to target language. We show that even though the quality of German system is worse than the quality of English one, this method allows to bootstrap a new language for the system very quickly and fully automatically.

## 1 Introduction

Every day news sources generates millions of news articles. News aggregation systems helps users to examine this overwhelming amount of information, combining thousands of article feeds into one feed of news events. The next evolutional stage of such systems are personalized news aggregators, which forms overall news feed based on users preferences.

News360 was created as one of these personalized news aggregation systems. Our crawler collects articles from tens of thousands of news sources, join them into clusters associated with news events and present them to user, ranking in order of her preferences. A brief description of modules of the system will be given in the section 1.1.

We have started working with English news articles and spent a lot of time improving our classification, clustering and personalization quality for users in USA, UK and other English-speaking countries. However, to further increase number of our users we had to add another language into system. So the problem was how to make our system multilingual and reach quality level for the new languages comparable with quality, that was already reached for English news. The approach proposed in this paper is fully automatic. Using it, we have successfully built German version of our system, which is already available for our users in Germany. Our approach allows us to easily add other languages and we expect that in a nearest year we will be able to work with 3-4 more European languages and probably one Asian. Before going into the details of the approach itself, we should describe our news article processing pipeline.

### 1.1 News360 Overview

News360 pipeline consists of 5 stages:

- **Crawling** articles from news sources, parsing them for text, attributes and metadata;
- **Named-entity linking (NEL)**;
- **Classification** and tagging news articles;
- **clustering**: group articles about same news event into one cluster;
- **Personalization**: retrieve results to users request, ranking them by a bunch of parameters, including users preferences.

We will not describe crawling, clustering and personalization stages here, because we assume them language independent (see section 1.4).

### 1.2 Named Entity Linking (NEL)

Named Entity Linking is the task of linking entities from some knowledge base to their mentions in the text. A lot of work in this field was done using open knowledge bases like DBPedia, Freebase



*Proceedings of the First Workshop on Computing News Storylines*, pages 35–39,
Beijing, China, July 31, 2015. 

or Wikipedia (see, for example, (Shen et al., 2015) for a survey).

NEL component in our system links mentions to entities in the manually curated ontology that was partly extracted from Freebase[1] and Crunchbase[2]. We have extracted only named entities: persons, locations, products and organizations. All mentions for an entity that were either extracted from an ontology or added manually are stored in the ontology as "synonyms" for an entity. During the processing of a news article, the system finds all the possible synonyms for all the entities in text. After that, all found objects are ranked by a set of hand-crafted rules. The structure and the evaluation of these ranking rules are out of the scope of this paper as we have turned off all rules that could be language dependent. Another component that we will not discuss here is the component that identifies unknown objects. Since it is rule-based and designed for English, it was useless in the multilingual scenario.

### 1.3 Classification

Apart from ontology, there is a wide tree of categories in our system. Total number is over 1000, and this number is increasing constantly. It includes both wide topics like "Space" and "Tech" and very marginal topics like "Microwaves" and "Blenders".

There are different modules that detect categories for an article in our system, each can add or remove[3] one or more category. The one that was most important for English articles was based on hand-crafted keywords, which, as we thought, could not be ported to other language fast. Another system was based on objects. It used automatically obtained mappings from objects to categories. We have set our hopes on this system because of its complete language independence.

### 1.4 Language (In)dependence

We have assumed that the only language dependent components of the system are linguistic components: NEL and classification, whereas other parts of the process, for example, personalization and clustering are language independent. This may be an oversimplification, because it is possible that language influences user preferences and expectations[4]. Still, we think that this question is not of paramount importance. We discuss this briefly in section 4.

Given this, the process of adding new language limits to this surprisingly small amount of steps:

- Implement Named Entities Linking to the objects in the ontology for the new language
- Implement classification process based on keywords to classify news articles in the new language

In the next sections we show that these two processes are sufficient to include news in any language to our pipeline. Section 2 is devoted to the problems we faced and decisions we made to overcome them. In section 3 we evaluate the system. In Section 4 we present our conclusions and discuss possible future improvements.

## 2 Methods of Extracting German Data

We have decided to employ the existing ontology for German instead of creating a new, unified ontology for both languages from scratch. For years of work, the ontology that we used was fine-tuned and upgraded, dumping all these changes would be unwise and would create a lot of bugs in the system.

### 2.1 Extracting German Data: Entity Linking

As it was already stated, to extract objects from English texts, our NEL component looks for every possible mention of any object in the ontology. These mentions are the "aliases" for entities, or "synonyms" as we call them. Since we have decided to use the ontology built for English articles, the only missing component were the synonyms for the target language. In order to extract them, we used several sources: Wikipedia dump, Freebase (Bollacker et al., 2008) and Wikidata (Vrandečić and Krötzsch, 2014) ontologies[5].

Since most of objects in our ontology were initially extracted from Freebase, links to the original Freebase entities were already known. Some of these objects in Freebase link to Wikipedia. On every step we have lost some fraction of objects: some objects in our ontology did not have a link to

[1] https://www.freebase.com/

[2] https://www.crunchbase.com/

[3] This is helpful sometimes to avoid presence of two controversial categories

[4] cf. Sapir-Wharf hypothesis of language relativity (Whorf and Carroll, 1956)

[5] When we started this project we have not know yet that Freebase was going to be discontinued. After the announcement, we added Wikidata to the list of our sources. We could not switch to it entirely since it had less data than Freebase

Freebase, some links has changed since the extraction, etc. Number of mapped entities, compared to the total number of entities in the ontology is presented in the table 1.

We also tried to map entities from our ontology with Wikipedia articles simply by their names and aliases, but mapping only by name showed low precision whereas mapping by aliases showed very low recall.

After establishing links from our ontology to Wikipedia articles we were able to extract possible object names from two different sources:

- Aliases for the object in Wikidata,
- Redirects to the object page in Wikipedia in target language.

Aliases were obtained by parsing JSON dump of Wikidata, the list of redirects were extracted with wikipedia-redirect utility[6]. Number of extracted synonyms are presented in the table 1.

| **Stage** | $N_{entities}$ | $N_{synonyms}$ |
|---|---|---|
| English | 662,462 | 5,008,436 |
| German | 111,126 | 278,964 |

Table 1: Amount of synonyms.

### 2.2 Extracting German Data: Classification

As it was said before, classification system based on hand-crafted keywords for every category was the most important. There were two ways of getting this system to work in German:

1. Porting existing keywords to another language;

2. Extracting keywords for another language automatically.

To port existing keywords we have decided to translate them automatically, using Yandex translation services[7]. Understanding that the translation would not be perfect, we have assumed that this is the most rapid way to approach an acceptable rate of classification quality for the new language. To further improve classification quality, we have tried to extract new keywords automatically. This process is described in the next section.

[6]https://code.google.com/p/wikipedia-redirect/

[7]https://tech.yandex.com/translate/

### 2.3 Various Sources of New Data

To extract keywords in the desired language automatically, we used Wikipedia as a corpus tagged by categories. Using Wikipedia categories as an approximate thematic markup, we mapped 80% of our topics to one or more Wikipedia categories. This way for every mapped category we have acquired a corpus which could be used to extract keywords. The topic was considered to be mapped on a Wikipedia category if the category contained the stem of the topic name as a substring.

After that one should determine keywords. We did not solve this task for topics which contained too little data from Wikipedia these texts, were used as a background corpus together with texts from topics which could not be mapped. We also ignored infrequent words. The first metric we used to score word relevance to topic was TF-IDF of given word in given topic, the second one was the conditional probability for text to be in the topic given that text contains the word.

As our most important categorization system is case sensitive, it is reasonable to take capitalization into consideration, especially for German. However, there is a risk to lose the word if it is specific for the topic but occurs in different capitalizations so as none of them look very important. Thus we counted TF-IDF for every form of every word and the second metric for lowercased forms. Words with the highest TF-IDF were marked as the keywords if their lowercase forms had high rank in the second list.

All these keywords got a moderate positive weight and gave the increase of categorization recall with no precision decrease, which caused a gain in F0.5-score for about 3%. Lowering a minimum threshold for word to be taken as a keyword gave nothing at first as they began to intersect with already existing sets but then gave drastic decrease of precision. See table 3 for details.

Using topic-specific N-grams should increase an impact of this method on the overall quality.

## 3 Experiments and Evaluation

### 3.1 Creating Evaluation Corpora

To evaluate the performance of the system on the new language, we had to evaluate system performance on English news articles first, since it was not done before. To do this, we have collected and marked up corpora. Our English corpus consisted of 100 non-random news articles, covering most basic categories: politics, sports, business, tech and so on. German corpus was smaller, it consisted of 24 non-random articles. Its size influenced its coverage: some important topics were not represented in the corpus at all.

Each article in each corpus was processed with the system and then fixed by hand by two experts independently. All inter-annotator disagreements in markup were settled. The procedure of corpora markup may have influenced the result: errors and focus of the system may have influenced the opinion of experts, but we will assume that possible error is insignificant, leaving this question for further research. Entities were marked up and linked to the ontology in each article, all possible topics were found for each article.

We have computed standard metrics for evaluation: precision and recall, but instead of using F1-measure as an average, we have chosen F0.5-measure (Rijsbergen, 1979). Precision is more important for the system than recall: showing something wrong to the user is much worse than not showing something.

Also, apart from measuring performance of the system on English and German, we measured it with so called "Emulated conditions": a system working with English while everything non-reproducible in German (or any other target language) was disabled. For example, the entity in the ontology was available in this setup only if it have been interlinked with an entity in target language (so we could extract synonyms for it). Using these conditions we could get approximate evaluation without corpora on the target language.

### 3.2 Named Entity Linking Task

The NEL component for German articles shows quality comparable to English given that there are six times less entities in German than in English in the ontology (as seen in table 1). The results for different setups are given in the table 2. Text was treated as a bag of non-unique objects: score for each object in corpus was the number of times the object was found in text divided by the number of object in corpus.

| Experiment | P | R | F0.5 |
|---|---|---|---|
| English | 0.938 | 0.662 | 0.866 |
| Emulated conditions | 0.849 | 0.607 | 0.786 |
| German | 0.790 | 0.422 | 0.673 |

Table 2: NEL evaluation.

### 3.3 Classification Task

Classification performs much worse than NEL (see table 3). Experiments (2) and (3) used language-independent classification components only, first of all categorization based solely on objects detected in texts. This method showed poor results probably because of types of objects in our ontology: they are all named entities, but not every category has a lot of named entities connected to it. Different categories vary in the average number of objects in texts, so this method works well only for a limited number of categories.

Categorization based on keywords, in contrast to the object-based method, behave quite unexpectedly: even when used with English keywords, it increases the quality of categorization drastically (4). Using keywords translated with machine translation increases the quality further (5). Methods described in section 2.3 allow to increase the quality further (6).

| Experiment | P | R | F0.5 |
|---|---|---|---|
| (1) English | 0.766 | 0.619 | 0.731 |
| (2) Emulated conditions | 0.545 | 0.189 | 0.396 |
| (3) German, no keywords | 0.429 | 0.058 | 0.188 |
| (4) German, English kw | 0.483 | 0.182 | 0.363 |
| (5) German, translated kw | 0.569 | 0.240 | 0.447 |
| (6) the same + new kw | 0.562 | 0.325 | 0.490 |

Table 3: Classification evaluation.

## 4 Conclusion and Future Work

We have showed that new languages can be integrated without great effort into systems similar to ours. Both NEL and classification modules show acceptable quality that are sufficient for launch.

Another result of this paper is the demonstration of applicability of machine translation to such unexpected tasks as providing keywords for classification.

One interesting topic that was left for further research is how appropriate it is to use the same ontology for different languages. It is possible that native speakers of two different languages would require two slightly different ontologies because of different way of thinking. Still, this approach is worse from engineering point of view: not only this is an unnecessary redundancy, this is also the possible source of undesired divergences in ontologies. So, despite the possible theoretical problem, having shared ontology seems more practical.

## References

Kurt D. Bollacker, Colin Evans, Praveen Paritosh, Tim Sturge, and Jamie Taylor. 2008. Freebase: a collaboratively created graph database for structuring human knowledge. In Jason Tsong-Li Wang, editor, *Proceedings of the ACM SIGMOD International Conference on Management of Data, SIGMOD 2008, Vancouver, BC, Canada, June 10-12, 2008*, pages 1247–1250. ACM.

C. J. Van Rijsbergen. 1979. *Information Retrieval*. Butterworth-Heinemann, Newton, MA, USA, 2nd edition.

Wei Shen, Jianyong Wang, and Jiawei Han. 2015. Entity linking with a knowledge base: Issues, techniques, and solutions. *Knowledge and Data Engineering, IEEE Transactions on*, 27(2):443–460, Feb.

Denny Vrandečić and Markus Krötzsch. 2014. Wikidata: A free collaborative knowledgebase. *Commun. ACM*, 57(10):78–85, September.

B.L. Whorf and J.B. Carroll. 1956. *Language, Thought, and Reality: Selected Writings of Benjamin Lee Whorf*. Language/Anthropology. Technology Press of Massachusetts Institute of Technology.

# Storylines for structuring massive streams of news

**Piek Vossen**
Faculty of Humanities
VU University Amsterdam
p.t.j.m.vossen@vu.nl

**Tommaso Caselli**
Faculty of Humanities
VU University Amsterdam
t.caselli@vu.nl

**Yiota Kontzopoulou**
Faculty of Humanities
VU University Amsterdam
p.kontzopoulou@gmail.com

## Abstract

Stories are the most natural ways for people to deal with information about the changing world. They provide an efficient schematic structure to order and relate events according to some explanation. We describe (1) a formal model for representing storylines to handle streams of news and (2) a first implementation of a system that automatically extracts the ingredients of a storyline from news articles according to the model. Our model mimics the basic notions from narratology by adding bridging relations to timelines of events in relation to a climax point. We provide a method for defining the climax score of each event and the bridging relations between them. We generate a JSON structure for any set of news articles to represent the different stories they contain and visualize these stories on a timeline with climax and bridging relations. This visualization helps inspecting the validity of the generated structures.

## 1 Introduction

News is published as a continuous stream of information in which people reflect on the changes in the world. The information that comes in is often partial, repetitive and, sometimes, contradictory. Human readers of the news trace information on a day to day basis to build up a story over time. When creating this story, they integrate the incoming information with the known, remove duplication, resolve conflicts and order relevant events in time. People also create an explanatory and causal scheme for what happened and relate the actors involved to these schemes.

Obviously, humans are limited in the amount of news that they can digest and integrate in their minds. Even though they may remember very well the main structure of the story, they cannot remember all the details nor the sources from which they obtained the story. Estimates are that on a single working day, millions of news articles are published. Besides the fact that the data is massive, the information is also complex and dynamic. Current search-based solutions and also topic tracking systems (Google trends, Twitter trends, EMM Newsbrief[1], Yahoo news) can point the reader/user to important news but they cannot organize the news as a story as humans tend to do: deduplicating, aggregating, ordering in time, resolving conflicts and providing an explanatory scheme.

In this paper, we present a formal model for representing time series of events as storylines and an implementation to extract data for this model from massive streams of news. Our formal model represents events and participants as instances with pointers to the mentions in the different sources. Furthermore, events are anchored in time and relative to each other, resulting in timelines of events. However, not every timeline is a storyline. We therefore use event relations (*bridging relations*) and event salience to approximate the *fabula*, or plot structure, where the most salient event (the climax of the storyline) is preceded and followed by events that explain it. Our implementation of the storyline extraction module is built on top of an NLP pipeline for processing text that results in a basic timeline structure.

The remainder of this paper is structured as follows. In Section 2, we present the theoretical background based on narratology frameworks which inspired our model described in Section 3. Section 4, then, explains our system for extracting storyline data from news streams according to the model. In Section 5, we report related works and highlight differences and similarities with respect

[1] http://emm.newsbrief.eu/NewsBrief/clusteredition/en/latest.html



*Proceedings of the First Workshop on Computing News Storylines*, pages 40–49,
Beijing, China, July 31, 2015. 

to our system. Finally, we discuss the status of our work, possible evaluation options and future work in Section 6.

## 2 What is a story?

Stories are a pervasive phenomenon in human life. They are explanatory models of the world and of its happenings (Bruner, 1990). Our mind constantly struggles to extract meaning from data collected through our senses and, at the same time, tries to make sense out of these data. This continuous search for meaning and meaningful patterns gives rise to stories.

In this paper, we make reference to the narratology framework of Bal (Bal, 1997) to identify the basic concepts which have informed our model. Every story is a mention of a *fabula*, i.e., a sequence of chronologically ordered and logically connected events involving one or more actors. Actors are the agents, not necessarily humans, of a story that perform actions. In Bal's framework "acting" refers both to performing and experiencing an event. Events are defined as transitions from one state to another. Furthermore, every story has a focalizer, a special actor from whom's point of view the story is told. Under this framework, the term "story" is further defined as the particular way or style in which something is told. A story, thus, does not necessarily follow the chronological order of the events and may contain more than one fabula.

Extending the basic framework and focusing on the internal components of the fabula, a kind of universal grammar can be identified which involves the following elements:

- Exposition: the introduction of the actors and the settings (e.g. the location);
- Predicament: it refers to the set of problems or struggles that the actors have to go through. It is composed by three elements: *rising action*, the event(s) that increases the tension created by the predicament, *climax*, the event(s) which creates the maximal level of tension , and, finally, *falling action*, the event(s) which resolve the climax and lower the tension;
- Extrication: it refers to the "end" of the predicament and indicates the ending.

Figure 1: Fabula or Plot structure

Figure 1 is a graphical representation of the internal components of the fabula.

Possible predicaments can be restricted to a closed set of high-level representations (e.g. the actor vs. society; the actor vs. nature; the actor vs himself; the actor vs. another actor), giving rise to recurring units and rules which describe their relations (Propp, 2010).

A further element is the hierarchical nature and the inherent intersection of stories. Multiple stories can be present in a single text and the same event, or set of events, may belong to different stories.

The model allows to focus on each its the components, highlighting different, though connected, aspects: the internal components of the fabula are event-centered; the actors and the focalizer allows access to opinions, sentiments, emotions and world views; and, the medium to the specific genres and styles.

These basic concepts and ingredients apply to every narrative texts, no matter the genre, such as novels, children stories, comic strips. News as a stream of separate articles, however, forms a special type of narrative that tends to focus on climax events on a routine basis (Tuchman, 1973): events with news value need to be published quickly while there may be little information on their rising action(s). At the same time, the falling action(s) and the extrication are not always available, often leading to speculation. Successive news articles may add information to the climax event explaining the rising action(s) towards the climax event and describing any follow up events when time passes.

In the following section we will describe our computational model and how it connects to these basic ingredients.

## 3 A computational model for storylines

Many different stories can be built from the same set of events. The starting point for a story can be a specific entity, a location, an event (Van Den Akker et al., 2011), from which time-ordered series of events spin off through relations that explain the causal nature of their order.

In our model we use the term *storylines* to refer to an abstract structured index of connected events which provides a representation matching the internal components of the fabula (rising action(s), climax, falling action(s) and resolution). On the other hand, we reserve the term *story* for the textual expression of such an abstract structure[2]. Our model, thus, does not represent texts but event data from which different textual representations could be generated. The basic elements of a storyline are:

- A definition of events, participants (actors), locations and time-points (settings)
- Anchoring of events to time
- A timeline (or basic fabula): a set of events ordered for time (chronological order)
- Bridging relations: a set of relations between events with explanatory and predictive value(s) (rising action, climax and falling action)

In the next subsections, we describe how we formalized these ingredients.

### 3.1 Mentions and instances

As explained in Section 2, a stream of news consists of many separate articles published over time that each give different pieces of information from different temporal perspectives (looking backward or looking forward in time) with partially overlapping information. We therefore first need to make a distinction between mentions of events and the unique instances of events to which these mentions refer. For this, we take the Grounded Annotation Framework (GAF, (Fokkens et al., 2014)) as a starting point. GAF allows to make a formal difference between mentions in texts and instances. Instances are modelled through the Simple Event Model (SEM, (Van Hage et al., 2011). SEM is an RDF model for capturing event data at an instance level through unique URIs. Following the SEM model, events consist of an action, one or more actors, a place and a time. A textual analysis detects mentions of these instances and their relations, where typically the same instance can be mentioned more than once. GAF connects the representation of these instances in SEM to the mentions in text through a *gaf:denotedBy* relation. Given the following text fragment:

> A380 makes maiden flight to US. March 19, 2007. The Airbus A380, the world's largest passenger plane, was set to land in the United States of America on Monday after a test flight. One of the A380s is flying from Frankfurt to Chicago via New York; the airplane will be carrying about 500 people.

We create an RDF representation in SEM with a single instance of a *flying* event through a unique identifier *ev17Flight*. Furthermore, it shows time, place and actor relations to entities identified in DBpedia:

```
:ev17Flight
rdfs:label "maiden flight", "test flight", "flying" ;
gaf:denotedBy
  wikinews:A380_makes_maiden_flight_to_US#char=19,25,
  wikinews:A380_makes_maiden_flight_to_US#char=174,180,
  wikinews:A380_makes_maiden_flight_to_US#char=202,208;
sem:hasTime wikinews:20070319;
sem:hasActor dbp:Airbus_A380, wikinews:500_people;
sem:hasPlace dbp:United_States, dbp:Frankfurt, dbp:Chicago,
 dbp:New_York.
```

The RDF structure provides a unique semantic representation of the event instance through the URI *:ev17Flight*, with `sem:hasActor`, `sem:hasTime` and `sem:hasPlace` relations to the participating entities that are also represented as instances through URIs. The `gaf:denotedBy` relations point to the offset positions in the sources where the event is mentioned. The participants in the event get similar representations with `gaf:denotedBy` relations to their mentions. Events and participants can be mentioned in different sentences and different news articles. Their relations are, however, represented in a single structure, a so-called *event-centric knowledge graph*. As such, GAF provides a natural way for resolving coreference, apply deduplication and aggregate information from different sources. In the above RDF example

### 3.2 Timelines

Instance representations for events require associating them to time. Such time anchors are minimally required to determine if two mentions of an

[2]Note that a storyline can be used to generate a textual summary as a story, comparable to (cross-)document text summarization.

event refer to the same event instance. Mentions anchored to different points in time cannot refer to the same event by definition. If no time anchoring is provided, we cannot determine the instance representation of the event and we are forced to ignore the event at the instance level[3]. Event timelines are thus a natural outcome of the model. Timelines are then sequences of event instances anchored to a time expression or relative to each other.

### 3.3 Towards Storylines

Given a timeline for a specific period of time, we define a storyline *S* as n-tuples *T, E, R* such that:

$$\mathbf{T}imepoints = (t_1, t_2, , ..., t_n)$$

$$\mathbf{E}vents = (e_1, e_2, ..., e_n)$$

$$\mathbf{R}elations = (r_1, r_1, ..., r_n)$$

*T* consists of an ordered set of points in time, *E* is a set of events and *R* is a set of bridging relations between these events. Each *e* in *E* is related to a *t* in *T*. Furthermore, for any pair of events $e_i$ and $e_j$, where $e_i$ precedes $e_j$ there holds a bridging relation $[r, e_i, e_j]$ in *R*.

We assume that there is a set of timelines *L* for every *E*, which is any possible sequence of events temporally ordered. Not every temporal sequence *l* of events out of *L* makes a good storyline. We want to approximate a storyline that people value by defining a function that maximizes the set of bridging relations across different sequences of events *l* in *L*. We therefore assume that there is one sequence *l* that maximizes the values for *R* and that people will appreciate this sequence as a story. For each *l* in *L*, we therefore assume that there is a bridging function *B* over *l* that sums the strength of the relations and that the news storyline *S* is the sequence *l* with the highest score for *B*:

$$S(E) = MAX(B(l))$$

$$B(l)) = \sum_{i,j=1}^{n} C(r, e_i, c_j)$$

Our bridging function *B* sums the connectivity strength *C* of the bridging relations between all time-ordered pairs of events from the set of temporally ordered events *l*. The kind of bridging relation *r* and the calculation of the connectivity strength *C* can be filled in in many ways: co-participation, expectation, causality, enablement, and entailment, among others. In our model, we leave open what type of bridging relations people value. This needs to be determined empirically in future research.

The set *L* for *E* can be very large. However, narratology models state that stories explain climax events through sequences of preceding and following events. It thus makes sense to consider only those sequences *l* that include a salient event as a climax and relate the other events to this climax event. Instead of calculating the score *B* for all *l* in *L*, we thus only need to build event sequences around events that are most salient as a climax event and select the other events on the basis of the strength of their bridging relation with that climax. For any climax event $e_c$, we can therefore define:

$$MAX(B(e_c \epsilon E)) = \max_{i=1}^{n} C(r, e_i, e_c)$$

The climax value for an event can be defined on the basis of salience features, such as:

- prominent position in a source;
- number of mentions;
- strength of sentiment or opinion;
- salience of the involved actors with respect to the source.

An implementation should thus start from the event with the highest climax score. Next, it can select the preceding event $e_l$ with the strongest value for *r*. Note that this is not necessarily the event that is most close in time. After that, the event $e_l$ with the strongest connectivity is taken as a new starting point to find any event $e_k$ preceding this event with the highest value for *r*. This is repeated until there are no preceding events in the timeline *l*. The result is a sequence of events up to $e_c$ with the strongest values for *r*. The same process is repeated forward in time starting from $e_c$ and adding $e_m$ with the strongest connectivity value for *r*, followed by $e_n$ with the strongest connectivity score *r* to $e_m$. The result is a sequence of events with local maxima spreading from $e_c$:

$$...e_k r_{max} e_l r_{max} e_c r_{max} e_m r_{max} e_n...$$

[3]In practice, we anchor so-called *timeless* events to the document-creation time by default or speculated events to a future time bucket

This schema models the optimized storyline starting from a climax event. By ranking the events also for their climax score, the climax events will occupy the highest position and the preceding and following events the lower positions approximating the fabula or plot graph shown in Figure 1.

## 4 Detecting storylines: Preliminary Experiments

In this section we describe a first implementation of our model and its steps for the storyline generation: a.) timeline extraction; b.) climax event identification; c.) rising and falling actions identification.

### 4.1 Extracting timelines

The timeline extraction is obtained from an NLP pipeline that has been developed in the NewsReader project[4]. The pipeline applies a cascade of modules, ranging from tokenization up to temporal and causal relation extraction, to documents (mention level). Next, it generates a semantic representation of the content in SEM (instance level). The NLP modules generate representations of entities mentioned in the text with possible links to DBpedia URIs, time expressions normalized to dates and a semantic role representation with events and participants linked to FrameNet frames and elements (Baker et al., 1998). Furthermore, coreference relations are created to bind participants and events to instances within each document. The NLP modules interpret mentions in the text, i.e. at single document level. However, given a set of documents or a corpus, these mention based representations are combined resolving cross-document coreference for entities and events, anchoring events to time and aggregating event-participant relations and generating an instance level representation. Details about this process can be found in (Agerri et al., 2014).

The timeline representation anchors events either to a time anchor in the document or to the document publication time. In case a time anchor cannot be determined or inferred, or if the resulting value is too vague (e.g. "PAST_REF"), the event is presented in the timeline but with an under-specified anchor such as `XXXX-XX-XX`. A natural result of this representation is a timeline of events, as described in (Minard et al., 2015). In Figure 2, we show an example of such a timeline constructed from the SemEval 2015 Task 4: TimeLine: Cross-Document Event Ordering[5] data. This representation differs from the Gold data of the task because it is "event-centered". This means that the events are ordered not with respect to a specific actor or entity. Each line corresponds to a time stamped event instance. Lines with multiple events indicate in-document event coreference. The first element of a timeline represents a unique index. Events with under-specified time anchors are put at the beginning of the timeline with index `0`. Simultaneous events are associated with the same index. Events here are represented at token level and associated with document id and sentence number.

```
3    2004-XX-XX    1173-3-deal       1173-2-deal
4    2004-03-XX    3307-10-purchased
4    2004-03-XX    3307-2-carry      3307-5-expected 3307-9-expected
4    2004-03-XX    3307-5-sales      3307-8-sales
4    2004-03-XX    3307-8-talks      3307-5-break
4    2004-03-XX    3307-9-flight     3307-4-flight   3307-9-flight
4    2004-03-XX    3307-9-take       3307-9-take     3307-3-take
4    2004-03-XX    4764-9-scheduled
5    2004-10-XX    1173-33-saying    1173-27-saying  1173-38-said
```

Figure 2: Event-centered Timeline

Although, all events may enter in a timeline, including speech-acts such as *say*, not every sequence of ordered events makes a storyline. The timeline structures are our starting point for extracting a storyline.

### 4.2 Determining the event salience

Within the set of events in a timeline, we compute for each event its prominence on the basis of the mention sentence number and the number of mentions in the source documents. We currently sum the inverse sentence number of each mention of an event in the source documents:

$$P(e) = \sum_{e_m = 1 \rightarrow N} (1/S(e_m)).$$

All event instances are then ranked according to the degree of prominence *P*.

We implemented a greedy algorithm in which the most prominent event will become the climax event[6]. Next, we determine the events with the strongest bridging relation preceding and following the climax event in an iterative way until there are no preceding and following events with a bridging relation. Once an event is added to a storyline it cannot be added to another storyline. For

[4] `www.newsreader-project.eu`

[5] `http://alt.qcri.org/semeval2015/task4/`

[6] Future versions of the system can include other properties such as emotion or salience of actors

all remaining events (not connected to the event with the highest climax score), we select again the event with the highest climax score of the remaining events and repeat the above process. Remaining events thus can create parallel storylines although with a lower score. When descending the climax scores, we ultimately are left with events with low climax score that are not added to any storyline and do not constitute storylines themselves.

For determining the value of the bridging relations we use various features and resources, where we make a distinction between structural and implicit relations:

- Structural relations:
  - co-participation;
  - explicit causal relations;
  - explicit temporal relations;
- Implicit relations:
  - expectation based on corpus co-occurrence data;
  - causal WordNet relation;
  - frame relatedness in FrameNet;
  - proximity of mentions;
  - entailment;
  - enablement.

Our system can use any of the above relations and resources. However, in the current version, we have limited ourselves to co-participation and FrameNet frame relations. Co-participation is the case when two events share at least one participant URI which has a PropBank relation *A0*, *A1* or *A2*. The participant does not need to have the same relation in the two events. Events are related to FrameNet frames if there is any relation between their frames in FrameNet up to a distance of 3.

In the Appendix A, we show an example of a larger storyline extracted from the corpus used in the SemEval 2015 Timeline task. The storyline is created from a climax event `["purchase"]` involving Airbus with a score of *61*. The climax event is marked with `C` at the beginning of the line. Notice that the climax event of this storyline is also reported in Figure 2, illustrating the event-centered timeline (`[4 2004-03-XX 3307-10-purchased]`). After connecting the other events, they are sorted according to their time anchor. Each line in Appendix A is a unique event instance (between square brackets) anchored in time, preceded by the climax score and followed by major actors involved[7]. We can see that all events reflect the commercial struggle between *Airbus* and *Boeing* and some role played by governments.

In Figure 3, we visualize the extracted storylines ordered per climax event. Every row in the visualization is a storyline grouped per climax event, ordered by the climax score. The label and weight of the climax event is reported in the vertical axis together with the label of the first participant with an *A1* Propbank role, which is considered to be most informative. Within a single row each dot presents an event in time. The size of the dot represents the climax score. Currently, the bridging relations are not scored. A bridging relation is either present or absent. If there is no bridging relation, the event is not included in the storyline. When clicking on a target storyline a pop up windows open showing the storyline events ordered in time (see Figure 4). Since we present events at the instance level across different mentions, we provide a semantic class grouping these mentions based on WordNet which is shown on the first line. Thus the climax event "purchase" is represented with the label more general label "buy" that represents a hypernym synset. If a storyline is well structured, the temporal order and climax weights mimic the fabula internal structure, as in this case. We expect that events close to the climax have larger dots than more distant events in time[8].

Stories can be selected per target entity through the drop-down menu on top of the graph. In the Figure 3, all stories concerning Airbus are marked in red.

Comparing the storyline representation with the timeline (see Figure 2) some differences can be easily observed. In a storyline, events are ordered in time and per climax weight. The selection of events in the storyline is motivated by the bridging relations which exclude non-relevant events, such as *say*.

We used the visualization to inspect the results. We observed that some events were missed because of metonymic relations between partici-

[7]We manually cleaned and reduced the actors for reasons of space.

[8]In future work we will combine the prominence with a score for the strength of the bridging and reflect this in the size.

pants, e.g. *Airbus* and *Airbus_380* are not considered as standing in a co-participation relation by our system because they have different URIs. In other cases, we see more or less the opposite: a storyline reporting on journeys by *Boeing* is interrupted by a plane crash from *Airbus* due to overgenerated bridging relations.

What is the optimal combination of features still needs to be determined empirically. For this we need a data set, which we will discuss in the next subsection.

### 4.3 Benchmarking and evaluation

In this phase we are not yet able to provide an extensive evaluation of the system.

Evaluation methods for storylines are not trivial. Most importantly, they cannot be evaluated with respect to standard measures such as Precision and Recall. In this section, we describe and propose a set of evaluation methods to be used as a standard reference method for this kind of tasks.

The evaluation of a storyline must be based, at least, on two aspects: informativeness and interest. A good storyline is a storyline which interest the user, provides all relevant and necessary information with respect to a target entity, and it is coherent. We envisage two types of evaluation: direct and indirect. Direct evaluation necessarily needs human interaction. This can be achieved in two methods: using experts and using crowdsourcing techniques.

Experts can evaluate the data provided with the storylines with respect to a set of reference documents and check the informativeness and coherence parameters. Following (Xu et al., 2013), two types of questions can be addressed at the *micro-level* and at the *macro-level* of knowledge. Both evaluation types address the quality of the generated storylines. The former addresses the efficiency of the storylines in retrieving the information while the latter addresses the quality of the storylines with respect to a certain topic (e.g. the commercial "war" between Boeing and Airbus). Concerning metrics, micro-knowledge can be measured by the time the users need to gather the information, while the macro-knowledge can be measured as the text proportion, i.e. how many sentences of the source documents composing the storyline are used to write a short summary.

Crowdsourcing can be used to evaluate the storylines by means of simplified tasks. One task can ask the crowd to identify salient events in a corpus and then validate if the identified events correlate with the climax events of the storylines.

Indirect evaluation can be based on a cross-document Summarization tasks. The ideal situation is the one in which the storyline contains the most salient and related events. These sets of data can be used either to recover the sentences in a collection of documents and generate an extractive summary (story) or used to produce an abstractive summary. Summarization measures such as ROUGE can then be used to evaluate the quality of summaries and, indirectly, of the storylines (Nguyen et al., 2014; Huang and Huang, 2013; Erkan and Radev, 2004).

## 5 Related Works

Previous work on storyline extraction is extensive and ranges from (computational) model proposals to full systems. An additional element which distinguishes these works concerns the type of datasets, i.e., fictitious or news documents, used or referred to for the storyline generation or modelization. Although such differences are less relevant for the development of models, they are important for the development of systems. Furthermore, the task of storyline extraction is multidisciplinary, concerning different fields such as Multi Document Summarization, Temporal Processing, Topic Detection and Tracking. What follows is a selection of previous works which we consider more strictly related to our work.

Chambers and Jurafsky (Chambers and Jurafsky, 2009) extended previous work on the identification of "event narrative chains", i.e., sets of partially ordered events that involve the same shared participant. They propose an unsupervised method to learn *narrative schemas*, i.e. coherent sequences of events whose arguments are filled with participants' semantic roles. The approach can be applied to all text types. The validity of the extracted narrative schemas (event and associated participants) have been evaluated against FrameNet and on a narrative cloze task: a variation of the cloze task defined by (Taylor, 1953). The narrative schema proposed perform much better than the simpler narrative chains, achieving an improvement of 10.1%.

McIntyre and Lapata (McIntyre and Lapata, 2009) developed a data-driven system for short children's stories generation based on co-occurrence frequencies learned from a training corpus. They generate story structure in the form of a tree, where each node is a sentence assigned with a score based on the mutual information metric as proposed in (Lin, 1998). The story generator traverses the tree and generates the story by selecting the nodes with the highest scores. Evaluation was carried out by asking to 21 human judges to rank the generated stories with respect to three parameters: Fluency, Coherence and Interest. The results have shown that the story generated by the system outperforms other versions of the system which rely on deterministic approaches. One relevant result from this work is the scoring of the tree nodes and the consequent generation of the story based on these scoring which aims at capturing the internal elements of the fabula.

Nguyen et al. (Nguyen et al., 2014) developed a system for thematic timeline generation from news articles. A thematic timeline is a set of ranked time anchored events based on a general-domain topic provided by a user query. The authors developed a two-step approach inter-cluster ranking algorithm which aims at selecting salient and non-redundant events. The topic timeline is built from time clustered events, i.e. all events occurring at a specific date and relevant with respect to the user query. The dates are ranked by salience on the basis of their occurrences with respect to the topic related events retrieved by the query. On top of this temporal cluster, events are ranked per salience and relevance. Event salience is obtained as the average of the term frequency on a date, while event relevance is a vector based similarity between the query and the time clustered document. A reranking function is used to eliminate redundant information and provide the final thematic timeline. The timeline thus obtained have been evaluated against Gold standard thematic timelines generated by journalists with respect two parameters: the dates and the content. As for the dates, the evaluation aims at comparing that the dates selected as relevant and salient for a certain topic are also those which occur in the Gold data. Mean Average Precision has been used as a metrics with the system scoring 77.83. The content evaluation determines if the selected events also occur in the Gold data. For this evaluation the ROUGE metric has been used, assuming that the generated timeline and the Gold data are summaries. The system scored Precision 31.23 and Recall 26.63 outperforming baseline systems based on date frequency only and a version of the system without the reranking function.

## 6 Conclusion and Future Work

We presented a computational model for identifying storylines starting from timelines. The model is based on narratology frameworks which have proven valid in the analysis of different types of text genres. A key concept in our model is the climax event. This notion is a relative one: each event has a climax score whose weight depends on the number of mentions and the prominence of each mention. Individual scores are normalized with respect to a data set to the maximum score. Next, storylines are built from climax events through bridging relations. In the current version of the system, we have limited the set of bridging relations to co-participation and FrameNet frame relations. Both relations are not trivial and pose some questions on how to best implement them. In particular, the notion of co-participation needs to be better defined. Possible solutions for this issue may come from previous works such as (Chambers and Jurafsky, 2009).

The set of proposed bridging relations requires further refinements both in terms of definitions and on their implementation. In particular, the big question is how to find the right balance between lexicographic approaches and machine learning techniques for identifying complex relations such as causations, enablement and entailment.

The preliminary results are encouraging although still far from perfect. Evaluation of the extracted storyline is still an open issue which has been only discussed in a theoretical way in this contribution. Methods for evaluating this type of data are necessary as the increasing amount of information suggests that approaches for extracting and aggregating information are needed.

The model proposed is very generic, but its implementation is dependent on a specific text type, news articles, and exploit intrinsic characteristics of these type of data. An adaptation to other text genres, such as fictitious works, is envisaged but it will require careful analyses of the characteristics of these data.

## Acknowledgements

This work has been supported by the EU project NewsReader (FP7-ICT-2011- 8 grant 316404) and the NWO Spinoza Prize project Understanding Language by Machines (sub-track 3).

## References

Rodrigo Agerri, Itziar Aldabe, Zuhaitz Beloki, Egoitz Laparra, Maddalen Lopez de Lacalle, German Rigau, Aitor Soroa, Antske Fokkens, Ruben Izquierdo, Marieke van Erp, Piek Vossen, Christian Girardi, and Anne-Lyse Minard. 2014. Event detection, version 2. NewsReader Deliverable 4.2.2.

Collin F Baker, Charles J Fillmore, and John B Lowe. 1998. The Berkeley FrameNet Project. In *Proceedings of the 17th International Conference on Computational Linguistics-Volume 1*, pages 86–90. Association for Computational Linguistics.

Mieke Bal. 1997. *Narratology: Introduction to the theory of narrative*. University of Toronto Press.

Jerome S Bruner. 1990. *Acts of meaning*. Harvard University Press.

Nathanael Chambers and Dan Jurafsky. 2009. Unsupervised learning of narrative schemas and their participants. In *Proceedings of the Joint Conference of the 47th Annual Meeting of the ACL and the 4th International Joint Conference on Natural Language Processing of the AFNLP*, pages 602–610, Suntec, Singapore, August. Association for Computational Linguistics.

Günes Erkan and Dragomir R Radev. 2004. Lexrank: graph-based lexical centrality as salience in text summarization. *Journal of Artificial Intelligence Research*, pages 457–479.

Antske Fokkens, Aitor Soroa, Zuhaitz Beloki, Niels Ockeloen, German Rigau, Willem Robert van Hage, and Piek Vossen. 2014. NAF and GAF: Linking linguistic annotations. In *Proceedings 10th Joint ISO-ACL SIGSEM Workshop on Interoperable Semantic Annotation*, page 9.

Lifu Huang and Lian'en Huang. 2013. Optimized event storyline generation based on mixture-event-aspect model. In *Proceedings of the 2013 Conference on Empirical Methods in Natural Language Processing*, pages 726–735, Seattle, Washington, USA, October. Association for Computational Linguistics.

Dekang Lin. 1998. Automatic retrieval and clustering of similar words. In *Proceedings of the 36th Annual Meeting of the Association for Computational Linguistics and 17th International Conference on Computational Linguistics-Volume 2*, pages 768–774. Association for Computational Linguistics.

Neil McIntyre and Mirella Lapata. 2009. Learning to tell tales: A data-driven approach to story generation. In *Proceedings of the Joint Conference of the 47th Annual Meeting of the ACL and the 4th International Joint Conference on Natural Language Processing of the AFNLP*, pages 217–225, Singapore.

Anne-Lyse Minard, Manuela Speranza, Eneko Agirre, Itziar Aldabe, Marieke van Erp, Bernardo Magnini, German Rigau, and Ruben Urizar. 2015. SemEval-2015 Task 4: TimeLine: Cross-Document Event Ordering. In *Proceedings of the 9th International Workshop on Semantic Evaluation (SemEval 2015)*, pages 777–785, Denver, Colorado, June. Association for Computational Linguistics.

Kiem-Hieu Nguyen, Xavier Tannier, and Veronique Moriceau. 2014. Ranking multidocument event descriptions for building thematic timelines. In *Proceedings of COLING'14*, pages 1208–1217.

Vladimir Propp. 2010. *Morphology of the Folktale*. University of Texas Press.

Wilson L Taylor. 1953. " cloze procedure": a new tool for measuring readability. *Journalism quarterly*.

Gaye Tuchman. 1973. Making news by doing work: Routinizing the unexpected. *American journal of Sociology*, pages 110–131.

Chiel Van Den Akker, Susan Legêne, Marieke Van Erp, Lora Aroyo, Roxane Segers, Lourens van Der Meij, Jacco Van Ossenbruggen, Guus Schreiber, Bob Wielinga, Johan Oomen, et al. 2011. Digital hermeneutics: Agora and the online understanding of cultural heritage. In *Proceedings of the 3rd International Web Science Conference*, page 10. ACM.

Willem Robert Van Hage, Véronique Malaisé, Roxane Segers, Laura Hollink, and Guus Schreiber. 2011. Design and use of the simple event model (sem). *Web Semantics: Science, Services and Agents on the World Wide Web*, 9(2):128–136.

Shize Xu, Shanshan Wang, and Yan Zhang. 2013. Summarizing complex events: a cross-modal solution of storylines extraction and reconstruction. In *Proceedings of the 2013 Conference on Empirical Methods in Natural Language Processing*, pages 1281–1291, Seattle, Washington, USA, October. Association for Computational Linguistics.

## Appendix A: Storyline Example

```
:Airbus

29      20040101 ["manufacturer","factory","manufacture"] :Boeing:European_aircraft_manufacturer_%2C_Airbus_%2C:Airbus
3       20041001 ["charge","level","kill"] :United_States_Department_of_Defense:the_deal
[C]61   20040301 ["purchase"] :People_s_Republic_of_China:Airbus_aircraft
23      20050613 ["win"] :European_aircraft_manufacturer_%2C_Airbus_%2C:Boeing
6       20050613 ["aid","assistance","assist"] :Airbus:Boeing:for_the_new_aircraft
1       20050613 ["spark"] :Airbus
15      20061005 ["compensate"] :Airbus:of_its_new_superjumbo_A380_%27s
22      20070228 ["cut","have","reduction","make"] :Airbus:the_company
39      20070319 ["supply","provide","resource","supplier","fund","tube"] :European_Aeronautic_Defence_and_Space_Company_EADS_N.V.
                                                                           :Airbus:United_States_Department_of_Defense

21      20070319 ["carry","carrier"]:the_airplane:Airbus_will
12      20070609 ["jet"]:Airbus:Airbus_A320_family
3       20070708 ["write","letter"]:Airbus:Boeing
21      20080201 ["ink","contract","sign"]:Royal_Air_Force:Airbus
13      20090730 ["lead","give","offer"] :France:Airbus
4       20041124 ["personnel","employee"] :Airbus:Former_military_personnel
20      20141213 ["carry","flight","fly"] :The_plane:Airbus
```

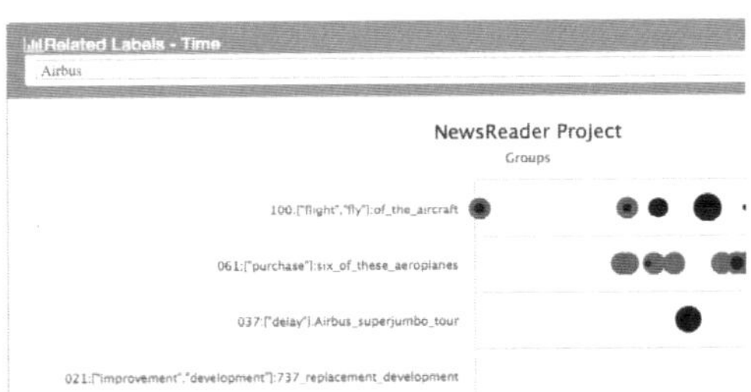


Figure 3: Airbus storylines order per climax event

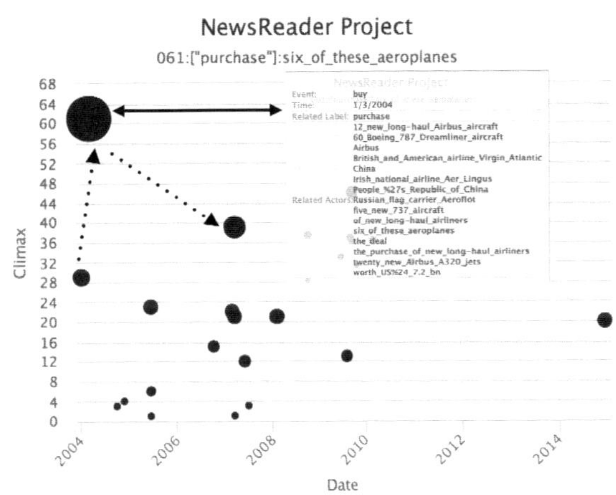


Figure 4: Airbus storyline for climax event [61] "purchase"

# From TimeLines to StoryLines: A preliminary proposal for evaluating narratives

**Egoitz Laparra, Itziar Aldabe, German Rigau**
IXA NLP group, University of the Basque Country (UPV/EHU)
{egoitz.laparra,itziar.aldabe,german.rigau}@ehu.eus

**Abstract**

We formulate a proposal that covers a new definition of StoryLines based on the shared data provided by the *NewsStory workshop*. We re-use the SemEval 2015 Task 4: Timelines dataset to provide a gold-standard dataset and an evaluation measure for evaluating StoryLines extraction systems. We also present a system to explore the feasibility of capturing StoryLines automatically. Finally, based on our initial findings, we also discuss some simple changes that will improve the existing annotations to complete our initial StoryLine task proposal.

## 1 Introduction

The process of extracting useful information from large textual collections has become one of the most pressing problems in our current society. The problem spans all sectors, from scientists to intelligence analysts and web users. All of them are constantly struggling for synthesizing the relevant information from a particular topic. For instance, behind this overwhelmingly large collection of documents, it is often easy to miss the important details when trying to make sense of complex stories. To solve this problem various types of document processing systems have been recently proposed. For example, generic and query-focused multi-document summarization systems aim to choose from the documents a subset of sentences that collectively conveys a query-related idea (Barzilay et al., 1999). News topic detection and tracking systems usually aim at grouping news articles into a cluster to present the events related to a certain topic (Allan, 2002). Timelines generation systems create summaries of relevant events in a topic by leveraging temporal information attached or appearing in the documents (Swan and Allan, 2000; Shahaf and Guestrin, 2010; Matthews et al., 2010; Mazeika et al., 2011; Do et al., 2012). TimeLines differ from other narrative structures like (Chambers and Jurafsky, 2008; Chambers and Jurafsky, 2009) in that the time-anchors of the events are required for Timelines construction. Although TimeLine systems present the sequence of events chronologically, linear-structured TimeLines usually focus on a single entity losing comprehensive information of relevant interactions with other participants. Thus, some other systems try to construct maps of connections that explicitly captures story development (Shahaf et al., 2013) or complex storylines (Hu et al., 2014).

Following this research line, we propose a cross-document StoryLine task based on the shared data provided by the workshop organizers. The approach extends the TimeLines evaluation task carried out in SemEval 2015[1] (Minard et al., 2015). The aim of the TimeLine task is to order on a TimeLine the events in which a target entity is involved (cf. Section 2). In contrast, our approach explores the inner interactions of these TimeLines. As a result, we define a StoryLine as a group of interacting TimeLines. For instance, given *Apple Inc.* as the news topic, Figure 2 presents a StoryLine built from *Steve Jobs* and *iPhone 4* TimeLines. It shows how an interaction of two TimeLines is highlighted when events are relevant to both TimeLines. In this way, a StoryLine groups together the events corresponding to multiple but interacting TimeLines. In the same way, if two additional entities interact with each other and they do not interact with *Steve Jobs* and *iPhone 4* TimeLines, two separate StoryLines would be derived from the *Apple Inc.* topic, each one corresponding to the set of interacting entity TimeLines.

The contributions of this research are manifold.

[1] http://alt.qcri.org/semeval2015/task4/



*Proceedings of the First Workshop on Computing News Storylines*, pages 50–55,
Beijing, China, July 31, 2015. 

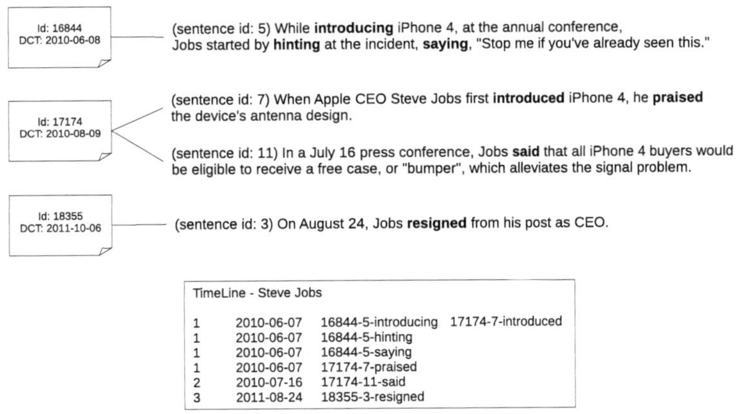


Figure 1: Example of the *Steve Jobs* TimeLine.

First, we devise a proposal that covers a new definition of StoryLines based on the existing proposal for TimeLines. We provide gold-standard StoryLines and we re-use the evaluation metric proposed in SemEval-2015 to evaluate StoryLines. We also present a very basic system that tries to capture the StoryLines that appear in the original documents of the TimeLines task. Finally, based on our initial findings, we discuss some initial improvements that can be addressed in the existing annotations and evaluation system to complete our initial StoryLine task proposal.

## 2 TimeLines

The aim of the Cross-Document Event Ordering task is to build TimeLines from English news articles (Minard et al., 2015). Given a set of documents and a set of target entities, the TimeLines task consisted of building a TimeLine for each entity, by detecting the events in which the entity is involved and anchoring these events to normalized times. Thus, a TimeLine is a collection of ordered events in time relevant for a particular entity.

Figure 1 shows the TimeLine extracted for the target entity *Steve Jobs* using information from 3 different documents. The events in bold form the TimeLine that can be placed on a TimeLine according to the task annotation guidelines (Minard et al., 2014). TimeLines contain relevant events in which the target entity participates as ARG0 (i.e agent) or ARG1 (i.e. patient) as defined in Prop-Bank (Palmer et al., 2005). Events such as adjectival events, cognitive events, counter-factual events, uncertain events and grammatical events are excluded from the TimeLine.[2] For example, the events *introducing*, *hinting* and *saying* from sentence 5 in document 16844 are part of the TimeLine for the entity *Steve Jobs* but the events *started* and *Stop* are not. *Steve Jobs* participates as ARG0 or ARG1 in all the events, but *started* is a grammatical event and *Stop* is an uncertain event. Thus, according to the SemEval annotation guidelines, they are excluded from the TimeLine. In addition, each event is placed on a position according to the time-anchor and the coreferring events are placed in the same line (see *introducing* and *introduced* events in documents 16844 and 17174 respectively).

The main track of the task (Track A) consists of building TimeLines providing only the raw text sources. The organisers also defined Track B where gold event mentions were given. For both tracks, a sub-track in which the events are not associated to a time anchor was also presented. The StoryLines proposal here presented follows the main track approach.

## 3 A Proposal for StoryLines

In this section we present a first proposal for a novel evaluation task for StoryLines. We propose that a StoryLine can be built by merging the individual TimeLines of two or more different entities, provided that they are co-participants of at least one relevant event.

In general, given a set of related documents, any entity appearing in the corpus is a candidate to take

[2] A complete description of the annotation guidelines can be found at `http://www.newsreader-project.eu/files/2014/12/NWR-2014-111.pdf`

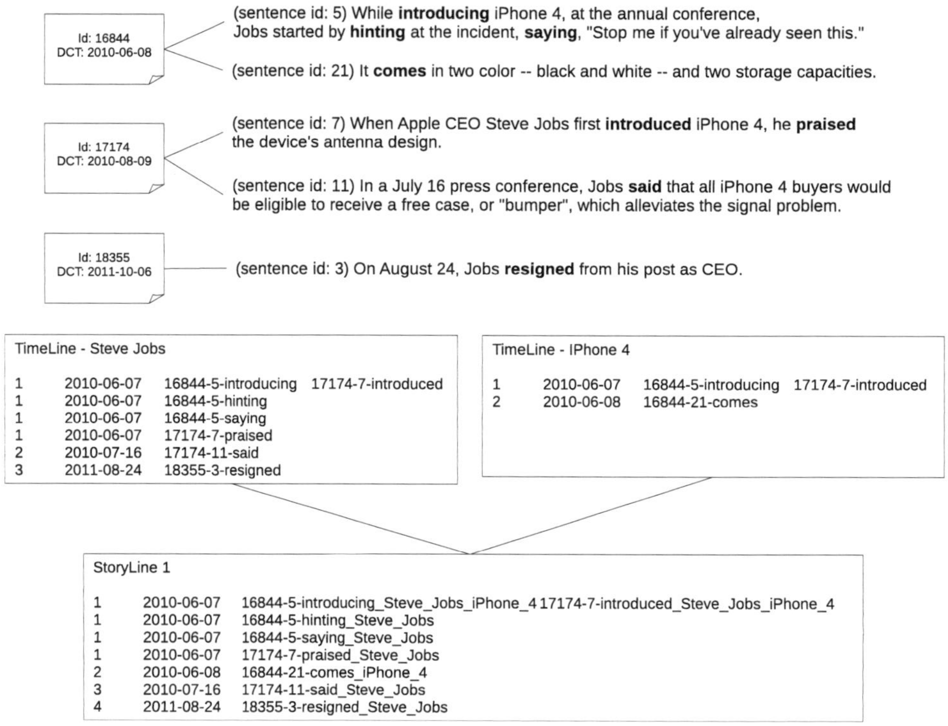


Figure 2: Example of a StoryLine merging the TimeLines of the entities *Steve Jobs* and *Iphone 4*.

part in a StoryLine. Thus, a TimeLine for every entity should be extracted following the requirements described by SemEval-2015. Then, those TimeLines that share at least one relevant event must be merged. Those entities that do not co-participate in any event with other entities are not considered participants of any StoryLine.

The expected StoryLines should include both the events where the entities interact and the events where the entities selected for the StoryLines participate individually. The events must be ordered and anchored in time in the same way as individual TimeLines, but it is also mandatory to include the entities that take part in each event.

Figure 2 presents graphically the task idea. In the example, two TimeLines are extracted using 5 sentences from 3 different documents, one for the entity *Steve Jobs* and another one for the entity *Iphone 4*. As these two entities are co-participants of the events *introducing* and *introduced*, the TimeLines are merged in a single StoryLine. As a result, the StoryLine contains the events of both entities. The events are represented by the ID of the file, the ID of the sentence, the extent of the event mention and the participants (i.e. entities) of the event.

### 3.1 Dataset

As a proof-of-concept, we start from the dataset provided in SemEval-2015. It is composed of 120 Wikinews articles grouped in four different corpora about Apple Inc.; Airbus and Boeing; General Motors, Chrysler and Ford; and Stock Market. The Apple Inc. set of 30 documents serve as trial data and the remaining 90 documents as the test set.

We have considered each corpus a topic to extract StoryLines. Thus, for each corpus, we have merged the interacting individual TimeLines to create a gold standard for StoryLines. As a result of this process, from a total of 43 TimeLines we have obtained 7 gold-standard StoryLines. Table 1 shows the distribution of the StoryLines and some additional figures about them. *Airbus*, *GM* and *Stock* corpora are similar in terms of size but the number of gold StoryLines go from 1 to 3. We also obtain 1 StoryLine in the *Apple Inc.* corpus, but in this case the number of TimeLines is lower. The number of events per StoryLine is quite high in every corpus, but the number of interacting events is very low. Finally, 26 out of 43 target entities in SemEval-2015 belong to a gold Story-

| | Apple Inc. | Airbus | GM | Stock | Total |
|---|---|---|---|---|---|
| *timelines from SemEval* | 6 | 13 | 11 | 13 | 43 |
| storylines | 1 | 2 | 1 | 3 | 7 |
| events | 129 | 135 | 97 | 188 | 549 |
| events / storyline | 129 | 67.5 | 97 | 62.7 | 78.4 |
| interacting-events | 5 | 12 | 2 | 11 | 30 |
| interacting-events / storyline | 5 | 6 | 2 | 3.7 | 4.3 |
| entities | 4 | 9 | 4 | 9 | 26 |
| entities / storyline | 4 | 4.5 | 4 | 3 | 3.7 |

Table 1: Figures of the StoryLine gold dataset.

Line. Note that in real StoryLines all interacting entities should be annotated whereas now we only use those already selected by the TimeLines task.

### 3.2 Evaluation

The evaluation methodology proposed in SemEval-2015 is based on the evaluation metric used for TempEval-3 (UzZaman et al., 2013) which captures the temporal awareness of an annotation (UzZaman and Allen, 2011). For that, they first transform the TimeLines into a set of temporal relations. More specifically, each time anchor is represented as a TIMEX3 so that each event is related to the corresponding TIMEX3 by means of the SIMULTANEOUS relation. In addition, SIMULTANEOUS and BEFORE relation types are used to connect the events. As a result, the TimeLine is represented as a graph and evaluated in terms of recall, precision and F1-score.

As a first approach, the same graph representation can be used to characterize the StoryLines. Thus, for this trial we reuse the same evaluation metric as the one proposed in SemEval-2015. However, we already foresee some issues that need to be addressed for a proper StoryLines evaluation. For example, when evaluating TimeLines, given a set of target entities, the gold standard and the output of the systems are compared based on the F1 micro average scores. In contrast, when evaluating StoryLines, any entity appearing in the corpus is a candidate to take part in a StoryLine, and several StoryLines can be built given a set of related documents. Thus, we cannot compute the micro-average of the individual F1-scores of each StoryLine because the number of StoryLines is not set in advance. In addition, we also consider necessary to capture the cases in which having one gold standard StoryLine a system obtains more than one StoryLine. This could happen when a system is not able to detect all the entities interacting in events but only some of them. We consider necessary to offer a metric which takes into account this type of outputs and also scores partial StoryLines. Obviously, a deeper study of the StoryLines casuistry will lead to a more complete and detailed evaluation metric.

### 3.3 Example of a system-run

In order to show that the dataset and evaluation strategy proposed are ready to be used on StoryLines, we follow the strategy described to build the gold annotations to implement an automatic system. This way, we create a simple system which merges automatically extracted TimeLines. To build the TimeLines, we use the system which currently obtains the best results in Track A (Laparra et al., 2015). The system follows a three step process to detect events, time-anchors and to sort the events according to their time-anchors. It captures explicit and implicit time-anchors and as a result, it obtains 14.31 F1-score.

Thus, for each target entity, we first obtain the corresponding Timeline. Then, we check which TimeLines share the same events. In other words, which entities are co-participants of the same event and we build StoryLines from the TimeLines sharing events. This implies that more than two TimeLines can be merged into one single StoryLine.

The system builds 2 StoryLines in the *Airbus* corpus. One StoryLine is derived from the merging of the TimeLines of 2 target entities and the other one from the merging of 4 TimeLines. In the case of the *GM* corpus, the system extracts 1 StoryLine where 2 target entities participate. For the *Stock* corpus, one StoryLine is built merging 3 TimeLines. In contrast, in the *Apple* corpus, the system does not obtain any StoryLine. We evaluated our StoryLine extractor system in the cases where it builts StoryLines. The evaluation results are presented in Table 2.

| Corpus | Precision | Recall | Micro-F |
|---|---|---|---|
| *Airbus* | 6.92 | 14.29 | 4.56 |
| *GM* | 0.00 | 0.00 | 0.00 |
| *Stock* | 0.00 | 0.00 | 0.00 |

Table 2: Results of the StoryLine extraction process.

Based on the corpus, the results of our strategy vary. The system is able to create StoryLines which share data with the gold-standard in the *Airbus* corpus, but it fails to create comparable StoryLines in the *GM* and *Stock* corpora. Finding the interacting events is crucial for the extraction of the StoryLines. If these events are not detected for all their participant entities, their corresponding TimeLines cannot be merged. For that reason, our dummy system obtains null results for the *GM* and *Stock* corpus.

However, this is an example of a system capable of creating StoryLines. Of course, more sophisticated approaches or approaches that do not follow the TimeLine extraction approach could obtain better results.

## 4 Conclusions and future work

We have proposed a novel approach to define StoryLines based on the shared data provided by the NewsStory workshop. Basically, our initial approach extends the pilot TimeLines evaluation task carried out recently in SemEval 2015. Our proposal defines a StoryLine as a group of interacting entity TimeLines. In particular, a StoryLine grups together the events corresponding to multiple but interacting TimeLines. Thus, several separate StoryLines can be derived from a news topic, each one corresponding to a set of interacting entity TimeLines.

As a proof-of-concept, we derive a gold-standard StoryLine dataset from the gold standard TimeLines provided by the pilot SemEval-2015 task. We also present a very basic system that tries to capture the StoryLines that appear in the original documents of the TimeLines task. As the same graph representation is valid for both TimeLines and StoryLines, we directly apply to our StoryLines the evaluation measure and system provided by the TimeLine pilot SemEval-2015 task. The gold StoryLines datasets are publicly available.[3]

Based on our initial findings, we foresee two major issues that need to be addressed. First, given a set of documents, the gold standard StoryLines require to annotate all the named entities participating in the StoryLine. That is, annotating the relevant events and entities interacting in the documents. Second, our proposal still needs to devise a more complete evaluation metric for properly evaluating StoryLines.

## Acknowledgments

We are grateful to the anonymous reviewers for their insightful comments. This work has been partially funded by SKaTer (TIN2012-38584-C06-02) and NewsReader (FP7-ICT-2011-8-316404), as well as the READERS project with the financial support of MINECO, ANR (convention ANR-12-CHRI-0004-03) and EPSRC (EP/K017845/1) in the framework of ERA-NET CHIST-ERA (UE FP7/2007-2013).

## References

James Allan. 2002. Introduction to topic detection and tracking. In *Topic detection and tracking*, pages 1–16. Springer.

Regina Barzilay, Kathleen R McKeown, and Michael Elhadad. 1999. Information fusion in the context of multi-document summarization. In *Proceedings of the 37th annual meeting of the Association for Computational Linguistics on Computational Linguistics*, pages 550–557. Association for Computational Linguistics.

Nathanael Chambers and Dan Jurafsky. 2008. Unsupervised learning of narrative event chains. In *Proceedings of ACL-08: HLT*, pages 789–797, Columbus, Ohio, June.

Nathanael Chambers and Dan Jurafsky. 2009. Unsupervised learning of narrative schemas and their participants. In *Proceedings of the Joint Conference of the 47th Annual Meeting of the ACL and the 4th International Joint Conference on Natural Language Processing of the AFNLP: Volume 2 - Volume 2*, ACL '09, pages 602–610, Suntec, Singapore.

Quang Xuan Do, Wei Lu, and Dan Roth. 2012. Joint inference for event timeline construction. In *Proceedings of the 2012 Joint Conference on Empirical Methods in Natural Language Processing and Computational Natural Language Learning*, pages 677–687. Association for Computational Linguistics.

[3] `http://adimen.si.ehu.es/~laparra/storylines.tar.gz`

Po Hu, Min-Lie Huang, and Xiao-Yan Zhu. 2014. Exploring the interactions of storylines from informative news events. *Journal of Computer Science and Technology*, 29(3):502–518.

Egoitz Laparra, Itziar Aldabe, and German Rigau. 2015. Document level time-anchoring for timeline extraction. In *Proceedings of ACL-IJCNLP 2015*, page to appear.

Michael Matthews, Pancho Tolchinsky, Roi Blanco, Jordi Atserias, Peter Mika, and Hugo Zaragoza. 2010. Searching through time in the new york times. In *Proc. of the 4th Workshop on Human-Computer Interaction and Information Retrieval*, pages 41–44. Citeseer.

Arturas Mazeika, Tomasz Tylenda, and Gerhard Weikum. 2011. Entity timelines: visual analytics and named entity evolution. In *Proceedings of the 20th ACM international conference on Information and knowledge management*, pages 2585–2588. ACM.

Anne-Lyse Minard, Alessandro Marchetti, Manuela Speranza, Bernardo Magnini, Marieke van Erp, Itziar Aldabe, Rubén Urizar, Eneko Agirre, and German Rigau. 2014. TimeLine: Cross-Document Event Ordering. SemEval 2015 - Task 4. Annotation Guidelines. Technical Report NWR2014-11, Fondazione Bruno Kessler. `http://www.newsreader-project.eu/files/2014/12/NWR-2014-111.pdf`.

Anne-Lyse Minard, Manuela Speranza, Eneko Agirre, Itziar Aldabe, Marieke van Erp, Bernardo Magnini, German Rigau, and Ruben Urizar. 2015. Semeval-2015 task 4: Timeline: Cross-document event ordering. In *Proceedings of the 9th International Workshop on Semantic Evaluation (SemEval 2015)*, pages 778–786, Denver, Colorado, June 4–5.

Martha Palmer, Daniel Gildea, and Paul Kingsbury. 2005. The proposition bank: An annotated corpus of semantic roles. *Computational Linguistics*, 31(1):71–106, March.

Dafna Shahaf and Carlos Guestrin. 2010. Connecting the dots between news articles. In *Proceedings of the 16th ACM SIGKDD international conference on Knowledge discovery and data mining*, pages 623–632. ACM.

Dafna Shahaf, Jaewon Yang, Caroline Suen, Jeff Jacobs, Heidi Wang, and Jure Leskovec. 2013. Information cartography: creating zoomable, large-scale maps of information. In *Proceedings of the 19th ACM SIGKDD international conference on Knowledge discovery and data mining*, pages 1097–1105. ACM.

Russell Swan and James Allan. 2000. Automatic generation of overview timelines. In *Proceedings of the 23rd annual international ACM SIGIR conference on Research and development in information retrieval*, pages 49–56. ACM.

Naushad UzZaman and James Allen. 2011. Temporal evaluation. In *Proceedings of the 49th Annual Meeting of the Association for Computational Linguistics: Human Language Technologies*, pages 351–356, Portland, Oregon, USA.

Naushad UzZaman, Hector Llorens, Leon Derczynski, James Allen, Marc Verhagen, and James Pustejovsky. 2013. Semeval-2013 task 1: Tempeval-3: Evaluating time expressions, events, and temporal relations. In *Second Joint Conference on Lexical and Computational Semantics (*SEM), Volume 2: Proceedings of the Seventh International Workshop on Semantic Evaluation (SemEval 2013)*, SemEval '13, pages 1–9, Atlanta, Georgia, USA.

# Cross-Document Non-Fiction Narrative Alignment

**Ben Miller**[♦], **Jennifer Olive**[♠], **Shakthidhar Gopavaram**[♣], **and Ayush Shrestha**[♥]
[♦]Georgia State University, Departments of English and Communication
[♠]Georgia State University, Department of English
[♣]Georgia State University, Department of Computer Science
[♥]IEEE Member
miller@gsu.edu, jolive1@gsu.edu,
sgopavaram1@student.gsu.edu, ayush.shrestha@gmail.com

## Abstract

This paper describes a new method for narrative frame alignment that extends and supplements models reliant on graph theory from the domain of fiction to the domain of non-fiction news articles. Preliminary tests of this method against a corpus of 24 articles related to private security firms operating in Iraq and the Blackwater shooting of 2007 show that prior methods utilizing a graph similarity approach can work but require a narrower entity set than commonly occurs in non-fiction texts. They also show that alignment procedures sensitive to abstracted event sequences can accurately highlight similar narratological moments across documents despite syntactic and lexical differences. Evaluation against LDA for both the event sequence lists and source sentences is provided for performance comparison. Next steps include merging these semantic and graph analytic approaches and expanding the test corpus.

## 1 Introduction

Changing patterns of news consumption and circulation such as disconnecting individual articles from their bundled newspaper sources, sharing individual articles, and the increasing velocity of article generation all require techniques for building ad hoc collections of articles on emerging topics (Caswell, 2015). Identifying articles that describe similar events could help answer this challenge and show the narrative similarity of those sections. However, these moments of similarity can occur in small sections of those articles. An approach with a highly granular focus that identifies a coherent piece of narrative, generates a structured representation of that narrative unit, and compares it against a corpus would aid readers' efforts to find and follow stories across articles. A coherent narrative textual unit describes a section of text that can be segmented from its surroundings while still describing a possibility, an act, and a result, a definition consistent with (Bal, 1997). Research on aligning these sections, or narrative frames, has been pursued in various domains (Prud'hommeaux and Roark, 2012)(Miller et al., 2015)(Reiter, 2014); this paper describes preliminary work extending that work to identify moments of narratological similarity but in the domain of non-fiction news articles.

To that end, we propose an expansion to a method for cross-document coreference of narrative units described in (Miller et al., 2015) that focused on the cross-document coreference of character and location entities. That method identified events in free text using EVITA (Saurí et al., 2005) then built adjacency matrices capturing entity-entity co-occurrence for each event. Similarity matrices were produced after combining the adjacency matrices and comparing the resulting story matrices using the Kronecker Product (Van Loan, 2000)(Weichsel, 1962) for sparse graph similarity measurements. Characters and locations were aligned by that method across stories based upon event-specific interaction patterns. This paper supplements that method with a process for better narrative segmentation and cross-document narrative correspondence identification. Frequently, these identifications lie four or more standard deviations from mean correspondence levels. These correspondences were found despite the narrative units crossing sentential boundaries, despite a high degree of semantic similarity across the corpus, and despite significant lexical and focal differences between the event descriptions. This work differs from other work in the domain of narrative/frame learning such as (Chambers and Jurafsky, 2009) in that it is sequence independent, does not connect entities and objects to roles, and focuses on discovering narrative situations for comparison rather than semantic role labeling. Like that example, the hypernym sequencing method described below does not rely on supervised techniques, hand-built knowledge, or pre-defined classes of events.

The test corpus is a set of articles related to Blackwater Worldwide. Blackwater (now Academi) is a private security company that has been contracted since 2003 by various American agencies to operate in Iraq. On September 16, 2007, Blackwater operatives killed 17 civilians and injured 20 more during an operation that went through Baghdad's Nisour Square. Articles on Blackwater approach their story from many angles. Some focus on the appearance of key Blackwater executives before congress. Others look to relate witnesses' perspectives on the massacre and contain translated quotes. Yet others summarize the trial that con-



*Proceedings of the First Workshop on Computing News Storylines*, pages 56–61,
Beijing, China, July 31, 2015. 

victed four of the firm's private security officers for crimes committed during that event. The heterogeneity of the articles' foci on that event prevented the cross-document linking of specific event descriptions based on lexical features or with topic modeling algorithms. That challenge and the articles' connection to human rights violations, a persistent interest of the authors, drove the choice of corpus.

## 2 Methodology

Comparison of narrative frames requires the production of structured representations. The graph similarity method from the prior work, and the hypernym sequence comparison methods operate in parallel to produce structured representations of entities on a per-event basis, and event similarity on a sliding window basis. Both processes begin with a set of $n$ articles to be segmented by event. This segmentation is done using EVITA as documented in (Miller et al., 2015). The result is a document segmented into a highly granular event sequence.

### 2.1 Event Segmentation and Direct Hypernym Sequences

EVITA uses statistical and linguistic approaches to identify and classify the language denoting orderable dynamic and stative situations (Llorens et al., 2010) and outperforms or is competitive with other event recognizers. EVITA's overall accuracy in event recognition was found by (Llorens et al., 2010) to be $80.12\%F\_\{\beta\} = 1$ over TimeBank with $74.03\%$ precision and $87.31\%$ recall.

Following granular segmentation, the key event word recognized by EVITA is lemmatized and a lookup is performed to WordNet for the word's direct hypernym. The word sense was chosen using the Simplified Lesk method (Vasilescu et al., 2004). Each event is automatically typified with a keyword from the source text, but not every keyword has an identified direct hypernym. If no hypernym match was returned, the event word is used; that substitution occurred for $16.3\%$ of the $5,422$ events. Sequences of hypernyms were built to encompass enough events to be commensurate with narratological theory of possibility, event, and aftermath (Bal, 1997). After experimenting with different length sequences, it was found that sequences of hypernyms that contained a number of events 3 times the average number of events per sentence, or approximately 3 sentences long, captured a span long enough to exemplify the theory but short enough to be distinct. In the case of this corpus, a preliminary random sample of 9 articles contained $2,112$ events in 464 sentences yielding an average of 4.55 events per sentence, which when multiplied by 3 to match the narrative theory of possibility, event, and aftermath, 13.65 events. Rounded up, our method yielded 14 events per sequence. Each sequence is offset by one event from the prior sequence, thereby producing a sliding, overlapping narrative unit window that goes across sentential boundaries. Two examples of generated sequences are provided in Table 1.

| Sequence Number | Hypernym Sequence |
|---|---|
| 209 | talk, blast, disappoint, prevent, veto, surprise, blast, act, injure, veto, label, cease, blast, injure |
| 210 | blast, disappoint, prevent, veto, surprise, blast, act, injure, veto, label, cease, blast, injure, inform |

Table 1: Example of two consecutive hypernym sequences from article 1.

### 2.2 Corpus

Our non-fiction corpus consisted of 24 news articles related to the September 16, 2007, shooting of Iraqi civilians by Blackwater security officers in Nisour Square, the investigation of the company's activities in Iraq prior to this incident, the outcome of those investigations, and the context of private security firms in Iraq. The subset are from 11 distinct international sources and were published between October 2007 and January 2011. Those articles were a random subset of the 616 articles returned by Lexis-Nexis for the following search: "Blackwater" and "shooting" with a length of $1,000 - 1,750$ words. That sample was selected as it contained a key focal event. All 24 articles were processed for the graph similarity method, and a smaller sample of 9 articles were used for testing the hypernym sequence matching method. Processing a larger sample is feasible as the hypernym sequencing method is entirely automatic but would require implementing $k$-means or $k$-nearest neighbors to help identify the correspondences.

### 2.3 Construction of Adjacency Matrices

Named-entity recognition (NER) and anaphora resolution was performed to establish entities in each event. Four raters performed overlapping manual entity extraction and resolution as current NER tools such as Stanford CoreNLP were not precise enough with multiword entities. NER and anaphora resolution lie outside the focus of this paper. Manual tagging was done according to an index of significant entities with corresponding unique reference codes. Significance was determined in the context of the corpus as entities mentioned multiple times across the corpus.

Using the entities listed in the index, individual event adjacency matrices were generated. These matrices record the presence or absence of entities in an event frame to show entity co-occurrence for every event. An example of a section of an adjacency matrix for article 1 is in Table 2. Each matrix is symmetrical with respect

| | BWSO | BWEX | IrVi | IrCi | NiSq | BaGZ | Bagh | USDOS | BWCO |
|---|---|---|---|---|---|---|---|---|---|
| BWSO | 0 | 0 | 0 | 0 | 0 | 0 | 0 | 0 | 0 |
| BWEX | 0 | 1 | 1 | 0 | 0 | 0 | 0 | 1 | 1 |
| IrVi | 0 | 1 | 1 | 0 | 0 | 0 | 0 | 1 | 1 |
| IrCi | 0 | 0 | 0 | 0 | 0 | 0 | 0 | 0 | 0 |
| NiSq | 0 | 0 | 0 | 0 | 0 | 0 | 0 | 0 | 0 |
| BaGZ | 0 | 0 | 0 | 0 | 0 | 0 | 0 | 0 | 0 |
| Bagh | 0 | 0 | 0 | 0 | 0 | 0 | 0 | 0 | 0 |
| USDOS | 0 | 1 | 1 | 0 | 0 | 0 | 0 | 1 | 1 |
| BWCO | 0 | 1 | 1 | 0 | 0 | 0 | 0 | 1 | 1 |

Table 2: Populated section of the co-occurrence adjacency matrix for article 1, event 53 (helping), from the sentence, "Prince disputed that, but said, 'If the government doesn't want us to do this, we'll go do something else.' Waxman also charged that the State Department acted as an 'enabler' for the company by **helping** it to cover up shootings and compensate victims"(Facts on File World News Digest, 2007)

to the number of entities identified in the articles. 12 events were extracted from the sentence and populated by 6 entities from the complete entity list and coding instructions as shown in Table 3.

| Code | Important Entities |
|---|---|
| BWSO | Blackwater Security Operatives |
| BWEX | Blackwater Executives |
| IrVi | Iraqi Victims |
| IrCi | Iraqi Civilians |
| NiSq | Nisour Square / The Traffic Circle |
| BaGZ | Baghdad's Green Zone |
| Bagh | Baghdad |
| USDOS | U.S. Department of State |
| BWCO | Blackwater |
| Witn | Witnesses |
| IrOf | Iraqi Officials |
| IrAg | Iraqi Agency |
| AmOf | American Officials |
| AmAg | American Agency |
| PrvSec | Private Security Firm |
| IrSf | Iraqi Security Forces |
| Iraq | Iraq |
| USA | United States |
| USMi | U.S. Military |

Table 3: Named entity list with codings

### 2.4 Creation of Similarity Matrices

With event hypernym sequences and event-specific adjacency matrices, we proceeded to determine similarity between narrative frames within our corpus. The adjacency matrix similarity measurement method used is as per (Miller et al., 2015), which was inspired by Blondel et al.'s HITS (Hyperlink-Induced Topic Search) algorithm (Blondel et al., 2004).

Hypernym sequence similarity of narrative units proceeded by pairwise comparison of all sequences across all articles. This process resulted in $2,188,573$ total comparisons that were scaled from $0$, indicating no overlap between sequences, to $1$, indicating identical sequences. This comparison was order independent (i.e. the sequence "a, b, c" is equivalent to "c, b, a") and is simply a measure of the number of overlapping terms.

Entity similarity measurement proceeded according to the methodology detailed in (Miller et al., 2015). That methodology builds a $3D$ matrix of the adjacency matrices where the axes from these individual matrices compose the first two dimensions and the event number composes the third dimension. Events are sequentially numbered 1 to $n$ on a per document basis. Those similarity graphs are then cross-factored using the Kronecker Product to assess possible cross-document entity-to-entity alignment. Our extension of that method to non-fiction intended to use that measure as a weighting factor for narrative unit alignment, but that procedure yielded a negative result as described below.

### 2.5 Evaluation

Comparison of the hypernym sequence matching method was done against LDA using Gibbs sampling for parameter estimation and inference. Sentences lemmatized with Stanford CoreNLP from the full corpus and the hypernym sequences from articles 1 to 9 were tested with both a 20 topic model and a 50 topic model using an alpha of $40/k$, a beta of $0.2$, and $2,000$ sample iterations. As this work is preliminary, no gold standard training data was produced for the comparison; topic model allocations were manually reviewed by three raters for coherence.

## 3 Preliminary Results and Discussion

Preliminary results revealed strong correspondences of narrative units across the corpus and suggests the viability of this method for cross-document narrative frame alignment. Negative results noted above in relation to the entity similarity measures suggest that it requires further development before application to non-fiction generally and news articles in particular.

### 3.1 Event Similarity

Comparing the degree of overlap of these sequences in a pairwise manner yielded a set of correspondence scores that were visualized with dissimilarity matrices as seen in Figure 1. High correspondence sequences were identified as those more than 3 standard deviations from the mean correspondence for each matrix. Discourse order of the hypernyms in the sequence is not considered by this process, as the system needs to be agnostic relative to aspects of focalization such as flashbacks or first-, second-, or third-person narration. Sentence groups encapsulating those sequences were returned via a lookup and manually verified.

Comparison of event sequences throughout the sample of the 9 articles within the corpus resulted in a comparison score mean of 0.212 with a standard deviation of 0.123 for $2,188,573$ total comparisons across 72 unique article comparisons. Values more than 3 standard deviations from the mean were found to correctly indicate similarity of narrative units. In part, this occurred because using the hypernyms of the event words tagged by EVITA generalized each event's description and allowed for more meaningful cross-document event alignment. Analysis of these significant similarity scores showed sequence matches in multiple articles. One example was found in articles 1, 6, and 7 within our corpus; the matching sequences are shown in Table 4.

Comparison of 6 and 7, as shown by the dissimilarity graph in Figure 1, found sequences 184 and 185 in article 6 and sequence 48 in article 7 as 0.857 similar. That graph is the pairwise comparison of each of the 227 sequences from article 6 (columns) against each of the 231 sequences from article 7 (rows). Values are color coded on as red to yellow to green along a 0-to-1 scale. Areas of similarity, such as the one just described that appears in the bottom left corner of figure 1, fade in and out of the background dissimilarity as the sequences move into increasing then decreasing alignment. Comparison of articles 1 and 7 found sequences 209 and 210 in article 1 and sequences 43, 44, 45, 46, and 47 as 0.786 similar. Rather than drop sharply, this high rate of similarity continues into sequence 48 of article 7 with a 0.714 similarity. The connection of these three similarity scores using article 7 as a vector for comparison indicates that the corresponding events are similar within each of the articles.

The original passages support this finding as each describes a car rolling forward, Blackwater security officers opening fire on the car, and subsequent fire on Iraqi civilians. The sentences from which these hypernym sequences were extracted are included in Table 4 with their associated article numbers and hypernym sequences.

### 3.2 Entity Similarity

Entity-to-entity graph similarity tests produced lower than expected similarity rates. These negative results,

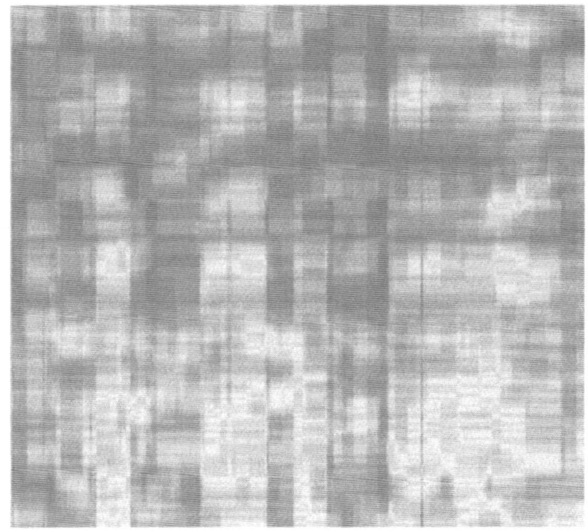

Figure 1: Dissimilarity graph showing the hypergram comparison across articles 6 and 7 using a color gradient scale where red indicates $< 50\%$, yellow indicates $50\%$, green indicates $> 50\%$ and up to $100\%$.

we theorize, occurred because non-fiction generally and news stories in particular feature more entities than fiction. That higher number of key entities led to more diverse entity co-occurrences and, therefore, more unique adjacency matrices. For our corpus, there were 27 unique entity sets with a mean of 6.6 occurrences per set and a standard deviation of 6.39. Without more significant overlap amongst the entity sets, the similarity analysis procedure yields sparsely populated graphs. The entity co-occurrences are too unique to compare with a large set of entities.

### 3.3 Findings

Despite the negative results in the entity similarity assessment portion, the core hypernym-based portion of this method correctly indicated cross-document similarity of narratives frames in a non-fiction corpus.

Most significantly, from a narratological perspective, the hypernym sequence model improved upon existing methodologies for cross-document narrative comparison in a manner consistent with narrative theory. This method operates at the clausal level, identifying the possibility, event, and outcome stages in a manner agnostic to sentential boundaries. This phenomenon can be seen in the similarity score between article 1 sequence 209 and article 7 sequences 43-47. As noted earlier, there is a slight drop in the similarity score as the narrative unit moves to sequence 48, which begins with the last events depicted at the end of a sentence: "Not one witness heard or saw // any gunfire coming from Iraqis around the square." In this example, the break between sequence 47 and 48 occurs at the "//", which was added for the purposes of this explanation. This slight decrease in similarity score and corresponding division of a sentence suggests that the events nar-

| Src. | Sq. | Hypernym Sequence | Source Sentence |
|---|---|---|---|
| 1 | 209 | talk, blast, disappoint, prevent, veto, surprise, blast, act, injure, veto, label, cease, blast, injure | "The shooting began at 12:08p.m., when at least one contractor began to fire on a car that failed to stop. The driver was killed and the car caught fire, but the contractors continued to shoot, killing the passengers and other Iraqis. At least one contractor reportedly called out to cease fire during the shooting, and another pointed his gun at a colleague" (Facts on File World News Digest, 2007). |
| 1 | 210 | blast, disappoint, prevent, veto, surprise, blast, act, injure, veto, label, cease, blast, injure, inform | |
| 6 | 184 | gunfire, express, perceive, perceive, blast, injure, express, blast, express, cut, affect, inspect, express, act | "All he saw, Sabah said, was that 'the white sedan moved a little bit and they started shooting.' As events unfolded and the Blackwater guards unleashed a storm of gunfire into the crowded square, Mr. Waso and Mr. Ali both said, they could neither hear nor see any return fire. 'It was one-sided shooting from one direction,' Mr. Waso said. 'There wasn't any return fire.' Mr. Waso said that what he saw was not only disturbing, but also in some cases incomprehensible. He said that the guards kept firing long after it was clear that there was no resistance" (Glanz, 2007). |
| 6 | 185 | express, perceive, perceive, blast, injure, express, blast, express, cut, affect, inspect, express, act, blast | |
| 7 | 43 | act, scat, injure, prevent, act, change_state, blast, injure, express, challenge, appear, injure, veto, talk | "The car continued to roll toward the convoy, which responded with an intense barrage of gunfire in several directions, striking Iraqis who were desperately trying to flee. Minutes after that shooting stopped, a Blackwater convoy – possibly the same one – moved north from the square and opened fire on another line of traffic a few hundred yards away, in a previously unreported separate shooting, investigators and several witnesses say. But questions emerge from accounts of the earliest moments of the shooting in Nisour Square. The car in which the first people were killed did not begin to closely approach the Blackwater convoy until the Iraqi driver had been shot in the head and lost control of his vehicle. Not one witness heard or saw any gunfire coming from Iraqis around the square" (Glanz and Rubin, 2007). |
| 7 | 44 | scat, injure, prevent, act, change_state, blast, injure, express, challenge, appear, injure, veto, talk, come | |
| 7 | 45 | injure, prevent, act, change_state, blast, injure, express, challenge, appear, injure, veto, talk, come, injure | |
| 7 | 46 | prevent, act, change_state, blast, injure, express, challenge, appear, injure, veto, talk, come, injure, suffer | |
| 7 | 47 | act, change_state, blast, injure, express, challenge, appear, injure, veto, talk, come, injure, suffer, perceive | |
| 7 | 48 | change_state, blast, injure, express, challenge, appear, injure, veto, talk,come, injure, suffer, perceive, cut | |

Table 4: Correspondences from articles 1, 6, and 7 with Hypernym Sequences and Source Sentences

rated in the first part of the sentence have a higher degree of similarity with sequence 109 in article 1. While the still significant score shows a relation between these two sets of sequences, it also shows the granularity at which the similarity assessments are made.

### 3.4 Future Work

While the automatic nature of the hypernym sequence comparison method will allow for it to scale, more sophisticated clustering techniques such as $k$-nearest neighbor will be needed to facilitate sequence similarity identification. Adapating the semantic role labling method from (Chambers and Jurafsky, 2009) might address the reliance of the graph simliarity method on insufficiently granular NER.

### 3.5 Evaluation

Evaluation of the hypernym sequence method against LDA proceeded as follows with the parameters as described above. The goal of this evaluation was to see whether the sequence method yielded more coherent clusters of meaningful narrative units. Each sentence was considered as one document. Using a java implementation of a Gibbs Sampling LDA method (Phan and Nguyen, 2006) on sentences that were lemmatized using Stanford CoreNLP, the corpus' $1,208$ sentences clustered into 20 topics with a mean of 78 sentences per topic and a standard deviation of 18.

Corresponding event sequences from the hypernym matching method did not perfectly align with the clustering of sentences proposed by LDA. In the three event-frame match across articles 1, 6, and 7, the hypernym method found a multi-sentence match across all three articles. LDA placed one of those sentences from article 1 and one sentence from article 6 in the same topic. Only one contributing sentence from each event frame was categorized into that topic. The surrounding sentences, though describing part of the same event, were identified as belonging to other topics. Briefly, narrative frames were not preserved – only semantic correspondences between individual sentences. LDA, by working at the document level, or in this case, at the sentence level, incorrectly preserves sentential boundaries in cases where narratives do not and does not allow for context to influence clustering. A narrative unit can begin in any clause of a sentence; tools for cross-document narrative coreference needs to work across sentential boundaries at the clausal level while still returning full sentence source texts to provide context. In our preliminary evaluations, LDA did not function as well as our hypernym sequence comparison.

## 4 Conclusion

Cross-document narrative unit similarity measurement is a promising area of research for the alignment of news articles. This successful preliminary work on abstracted event-keyword comparison based on event segmentation worked well in finding multi-sentence, statistically significant narrative unit correspondences across a small corpus of related articles. Extensions of an existing method for narrative alignment using graph similarity measures were not successful. We theorize this result because of the greater number of entities and intra-event entity sets that occur in non-fiction news reporting than in fiction. Future work looks to use the hypernym sequence comparison method to cluster events into narrative units, and then apply the entity co-occurrence method as a weighting factor for similarity measurement. While automatic NER would facilitate the integration of these two methods, a manual approach that focuses on the high similarity sections might curtail the task sufficiently to allow for it to remain feasible as the corpus size increases. We also plan to integrate $k$-means clustering into the analytic pipeline to facilitate identification of corresponding narrative units.

## Acknowledgments

This work is supported in part by NSF award 1209172. We thank the reviewers for their helpful suggestions.

## References


Mieke Bal. 1997. *Narratology: Introduction to the theory of narrative*. University of Toronto Press.

Vincent D. Blondel, Anahí Gajardo, Maureen Heymans, Pierre Senellart, and Paul Van Dooren. 2004. A measure of similarity between graph vertices: Applications to synonym extraction and web searching. *SIAM review*, 46(4):647–666.

DA Caswell. 2015. Structured narratives as a framework for journalism: A work in progress. In *Proceedings of the 6th Workshop on Computational Models of Narrative (CMN 2015)*.

Nathanael Chambers and Dan Jurafsky. 2009. Unsupervised learning of narrative schemas and their participants. In *Proceedings of the Joint Conference of the 47th Annual Meeting of the ACL and the 4th International Joint Conference on Natural Language Processing of the AFNLP: Volume 2-Volume 2*, pages 602–610. Association for Computational Linguistics.

Hector Llorens, Estela Saquete, and Borja Navarro-Colorado. 2010. Timeml events recognition and classification: learning crf models with semantic roles. In *Proceedings of the 23rd International Conference on Computational Linguistics*, pages 725–733. Association for Computational Linguistics.

Ben Miller, Ayush Shrestha, Jennifer Olive, and Shakthidhar Gopavaram. 2015. Cross-document narrative frame alignment. In *2015 Workshop on Computational Models of Narrative*, volume 42, page forthcoming.

Xuan-Hieu Phan and Cam-Tu Nguyen. 2006. Jgibblda: A java implementation of latent dirichlet allocation (lda) using gibbs sampling for parameter estimation and inference.

Emily T Prud'hommeaux and Brian Roark. 2012. Graph-based alignment of narratives for automated neurological assessment. In *Proceedings of the 2012 Workshop on Biomedical Natural Language Processing*, pages 1–10. Association for Computational Linguistics.

Nils Reiter. 2014. Discovering structural similarities in narrative texts using event alignment algorithms.

Roser Saurí, Robert Knippen, Marc Verhagen, and James Pustejovsky. 2005. Evita: a robust event recognizer for qa systems. In *Proceedings of the conference on Human Language Technology and Empirical Methods in Natural Language Processing*, pages 700–707. Association for Computational Linguistics.

Charles F Van Loan. 2000. The ubiquitous kronecker product. *Journal of computational and applied mathematics*, 123(1):85–100.

Florentina Vasilescu, Philippe Langlais, and Guy Lapalme. 2004. Evaluating variants of the lesk approach for disambiguating words.

Paul M Weichsel. 1962. The kronecker product of graphs. *Proceedings of the American Mathematical Society*, 13(1):47–52.

# Author Index

**Association for Computational Linguistics**
209 N. Eighth Street
Stroudsburg, Pennsylvania 18360

ISBN 978-1-5108-0952-9

CURRAN ASSOCIATES INC.
proceedings.com